DAVID J. ALLEN AND ~~PATRICK~~ IMRIE

Discovering
The North Downs
Way

SHIRE PUBLICATIONS LTD

Contents

Set in 9 point Times by Oxford Publishing Services and printed in Great Britain by C. I. Thomas & Sons (Haverfordwest) Ltd, Press Buildings, Merlins Bridge, Haverfordwest.

Introduction

The North Downs Way runs for over 140 miles from Farnham in Surrey to Dover in Kent. First proposed by the Countryside Commission in 1963, it received government approval in 1969. However, 36 miles of new rights of way had to be negotiated and it was not until September 1978 that the Way was officially opened by the Archbishop of Canterbury at a ceremony held in Wye. Even now, rights have not been negotiated over the entire length and a few sections exist where temporary links have had to be established.

The path runs, as far as possible, along the almost unbroken ridge of chalk which stretches from Farnham to Dover and gives many extensive views. The countryside through which the way passes is extremely attractive as the path is almost completely contained within the Surrey Hills and Kent Downs Areas of Outstanding Natural Beauty. Although a glance at any map of the area will show that the Way passes by some of the most heavily populated areas of Britain, it is remarkable how remote much of the path appears to be.

In some sections between Farnham and Canterbury the route coincides with the Pilgrims' Way, which is supposedly the route taken by medieval pilgrims from Winchester to Canterbury. After the murder of Thomas à Becket in 1170 Canterbury became, after Rome, the major place of pilgrimage in Christendom. Winchester was also a holy city (it boasted the shrine of St Swithun) and had only comparatively recently been succeeded by London as the capital. Many continental pilgrims would have congregated at Winchester after arriving at the ports along the Solent. However, some authorities argue that the Pilgrims' Way is more of a modern romantic fancy than an historical roadway. It is certain, though, that some of the travellers who flocked to the shrine of St Thomas would have used the very ancient trackways along the North Downs. There is some evidence of the importance of this route in that several churches along it appear to have housed holy relics and have been adapted to allow large numbers of visitors to view them. After the decline in the pilgrimages the trackways were often used as drove roads and the introduction of the turnpike system made them attractive to those who wished to avoid the tolls. The line of the North Downs Way was mainly chosen for its scenic qualities and this means that the Pilgrims' Way is often found lower down the slope.

Although the Way was chosen more for its scenery than historical associations, there are many places and sites of interest on or near the path. The safe Channel ports, close to the Continent, and the gentler climate made it inevitable that the southern counties, and Kent in particular, should have been settled by successive

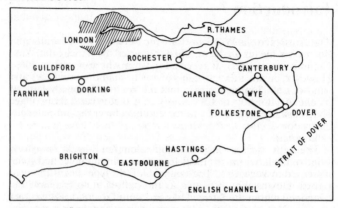

races. Much of the history of Britain is represented along the Way in buildings ranging from neolithic tombs, Roman villas, Norman churches and castles, right up to the present with views of hover-ports and a nuclear power station. One of the bonuses of the North Downs Way is that not only does it provide good walking in very attractive countryside but it is surrounded by places of interest which are well worthwhile making short detours to see. Some of the churches may be locked, but it is usually possible to obtain the key fairly easily.

For the most part the walking is very easy and pleasant and whether you are a long-distance walker or out for an afternoon stroll the Way has much to offer. Although the walking is easy, sensible shoes are always advisable, particularly as parts of the path are also bridleways and can be muddy even in summer.

We have divided the route into twenty-five walking sections and have included separate sections on Farnham and Dover and the three cathedral cities, Guildford, Rochester and Canterbury. The walking sections range in length from about 4 to 8 miles and have been chosen to begin and end at convenient access points. However, there is good access to most parts of the path and it is, of course, possible to join and leave it at other points and vary the length of walk to individual requirements. Public transport facilities near the Way are on the whole good and we have included an outline of bus and train services in each section. However, bus services in particular are not necessarily daily and it is sensible to check before setting out. It is perfectly possible, however, to walk the entire path as a series of day excursions from most places. Roadside parking is possible near much of the route and in addition several car parks exist and are marked on the maps.

Accommodation should be no problem as you are within easy

4

reach of most towns near the Way. There are a number of publications available listing the facilities in the area.

Refreshments also should be no problem. We have listed some, but by no means all, of the public houses on or near the Way. Many pubs can provide some food but where we have noted (Food) it means they offer more variety than the usual pies and sandwiches. However, one cannot rely on food being available at weekends. It is also worth remembering that in rural areas village shops usually close at lunchtime and may be closed on Saturday afternoons.

Waymarking is at present quite good along the Way. In Surrey the route is marked with oak signposts and in Kent by low stone plinths, the latter having the disadvantage of sometimes becoming obscured by vegetation in the summer. Both types bear the words 'North Downs Way' and the acorn symbol. In some places the acorn waymark is used to confirm the route. No doubt as time goes by the waymarks will suffer from vandalism and if you notice any damage to them or stiles, or obstructions to the path, please notify the appropriate county council which is responsible for the maintenance of the Way. We hope that it is not necessary to remind you to shut gates and generally remember the Country Code.

Notes on the maps

The sketch maps are drawn approximately to scale and are intended to show the route of the Way and features and places of interest on or near it. Other roads and places marked are merely intended for orientation and are not necessarily complete or shown in strictly accurate locations. The depiction of a road or track does not necessarily imply there is public access.

The position of most waymarks, gates and stiles is shown, but on a small-scale map it is impossible to mark all of them, particularly when two or more occur in short succession. They should not, therefore, be used as an indication of the position reached on the Way. The Ordnance Survey 1:50,000 maps which cover the North Downs Way are numbers 178, 179, 186, 187, 188 and 189.

Acknowledgements

We are grateful to Margaret and Debbie Allen and Susanne Imrie for their companionship on the walk; to Margaret Allen for advice and criticism on the manuscript and to Susanne Imrie for typing it. We also thank the friends who have helped in many ways.

The cover photograph of Trottiscliffe is by Cadbury Lamb.

———————	North Downs Way
• • • • • • • • •	Designated Route
═══════════	Surfaced Road
- - - - - - - - -	Unsurfaced Road (Track)
- - - - - - - - -	Footpath
┼┼┼┼┼●┼┼┼┼┼	Railway line & Station
┼┼┼┼┼┼┼┼┼┼	Disused Railway
～━●━～	River & Lake
W G S	Waymark, Gate, Stile
⌀	Church or Chapel
Ⓟ	Car Park
▲ Y.H.	Youth Hostel
■	Building
●	Site of Interest
⁖⁙	Castle or Fort
P.H.	Public House

Key to maps

The National Register of Long Distance Paths, 8 Upton Grey Close, Winchester, Hampshire SO22 6NE, provides an advisory service for those involved with the development of new or existing long-distance paths.

Farnham

Tourist information: South Street (telephone: Godalming 4014, ext 214/5).
Buses: services to Guildford etc; frequent service to London from Castle Street.
Trains: to Alton or Woking and London (Waterloo); telephone enquiries, Basingstoke 64966 or Woking 65251.
Places of interest: Farnham Museum, 38 West Street (telephone: Farnham 5094); open Tuesday to Saturday, 11–1 and 2–5 (mid November to mid February 10.30–1 and 2–4.30), Sunday and Bank Holidays, 2–5 (mid November to mid February 2.30–4.30); Farnham Castle, Keep open April to September, Great Hall and other rooms, open Wednesday 2–4.

Farnham sits in a hollow that provides a natural nexus for old roads. To the east lie the North Downs, over which the earliest travellers came to Britain from the Straits of Dover and, later, pilgrims journeyed to Canterbury. Westwards ran the Old Hoar Way to Stonehenge and the south-west, with its wealth of metal that so attracted prehistoric man. It was also the obvious line for the north-south road from London to Winchester and the good ports along the Solent.

Archaeological remains from every period of prehistory have been discovered in the district and the early importance of the area is indicated by the finding of seven Romano-British potteries in the town. In AD 688 the king of the West Saxons, Caedwella, gave sixty hides of land at Fearnhamme (water meadows at river bend among ferns) for a Christian church. In the ninth century Farnham became part of the See of Winchester and it has been an important centre since then.

On the side of the modern police station there are illustrations of the Bishops of Winchester, of hop growing and of wheat harvesting, which between them until recent times were the town's principal sources of wealth. Aubrey wrote in his *Perambulation of Surrey* in the 1600s that the town was the greatest market in England for wheat and also 'good for oats, and a great market for Welsh stockings'.

There are many fine buildings to see, including a number of old inns. The Bush Hotel, with entrances in South Street and The Borough, is mentioned by Thackeray in *The Virginians*. Further along The Borough is the timber-framed Spinning Wheel, now housing a shoe shop. In West Street stands the Lion and Lamb, which dates from 1537, now tea rooms and printing offices, with a charming courtyard behind.

Further along West Street is Vernon House, now the public library. It was renovated in 1727 but the original was sixteenth-century. Charles I on the way to his trial in London stayed here and met the Roundhead general Thomas Harris, who later signed his death warrant. Just past Vernon House is Willmer House, now the town museum, built in 1718, with a fine cut brick facade. It takes its name from Miss Willmer's boarding school for girls, which it housed in the early nineteenth century. Number 10 West Street was the birthplace of Augustus Toplady, who wrote the hymn 'Rock of Ages'.

Castle Street, facing the Spinning Wheel, is very broad and typical of streets that were used for markets. At 75 Castle Street stood the Farnham Bank, which issued its own banknotes, specimens of which can be seen in the museum. Numbers 53–60, next to the Nelson Arms, are a group of almshouses built in 1619, as a notice declares, for '8 poor, old, honest, impotent persons'.

At the top of Castle Street steps lead up to the castle, some of it stone but much of it again built in red brick. There were, almost certainly, a mound and earthworks here in Saxon times but the oldest visible masonry is that surviving from the castle Bishop Blois built in 1138 during the fighting over the throne between the Empress Matilda and King Stephen. Matilda's son, Henry II, took advantage of the absence of de Blois (who was Stephen's brother) in France to destroy it but it was soon rebuilt in a rather different form. Bishop Fox (1500–28) strengthened the gateway to the keep, and most of the present buildings were built by Bishop Morley (1662–84).

Farnham and Guildford castles were captured in a single day by Louis, the Dauphin of France, when he was invited over in 1216 by barons disenchanted with King John. In the first few weeks of the Civil War the governor was George Wither, a fiery puritan and poet, but he was soon driven out by the local people. By a strange coincidence he was replaced by another poet, Sir John Denham, the High Sheriff of Surrey. Denham is reputed to have pleaded that Wither's life might be saved so that he, Sir John Denham, might not be the worst poet alive. Later the Parliamentarians, under Sir William Waller, captured and partly destroyed the castle. Until 1926 the castle remained the residence of the Bishops of Winchester and then until 1956 that of the Bishops of Guildford. Today parts of it are used as a Centre for International Briefing.

The large and airy parish church of St Andrew, in Downing Street, is partly Norman and Early English but mainly dates from the fourteenth and fifteenth centuries. It was extensively restored in 1855. Just outside the main door is the grave of William Cobbett and his wife Anne and, alongside, his father and grandfather. Of his prolific writing the best known is *Rural Rides*, an account of his travels through southern England in the early nineteenth century, much influenced by his political and other strong opinions. He was also the founder of parliamentary reports, still called after the printer he chose, Luke Hansard. He was born in 1762 in the house that is now a public house, the William Cobbett (previously the Jolly Farmers), in Bridge Square just south of the river Wey.

On the opposite side of the road from the William Cobbett are the Maltings, whose early nineteenth-century buildings have been converted for use as a community centre. A little way along the river are the Haren Gardens and the traffic lights at the end of South Street. The railway station is up Station Hill to the right. From this junction the start of the North Downs Way is a few yards along the bypass (A31).

1. Farnham to Puttenham

Buses: Puttenham and The Sands to Farnham.
Parking: Farnham; opposite the Jolly Farmers at Puttenham.
Pubs: numerous in Farnham, including the Bluebell Hotel (restaurant, bar food, garden) near the railway station; Barley Mow at The Sands; Good Intent, Jolly Farmers (restaurant) at Puttenham.
Toilets: Haren Gardens, Farnham.

The start of the North Downs Way is off the A31 (Farnham Bypass) up a track that soon runs alongside the river Wey. It passes an attractive farmhouse and then turns right under the railway at The Kiln (an interesting conversion to a private house of an industrial building) into a path beside flat meadows close to the river.

In ¼ mile, above Culverlands, the Way turns right beside a paddock to go up to a road. It turns into Compton Way, a few yards to the left, and crosses the river and passes Moor Park College. The original house, built in 1630, was altered in 1684 for Sir William Temple, the noted diplomat. Jonathan Swift came to the house as Sir William's secretary and wrote *The Tale of a Tub* there. He became tutor to Esther Johnson (then an eight-year-old girl), whom he called Stella. At the far end of the grounds a cave, St Mary's Well, was once occupied by a notorious witch, Mother Ludlam. Later, in the nineteenth century, a hermit, previously a rich businessman, lived in it for eleven years in disgusting squalor.

Close by is Waverley Abbey, the oldest Cistercian monastery in Britain. After the dissolution Sir William More used much of the stone to build Loseley House. Reading the abbey's annals gave Sir Walter Scott the name for his *Waverley* novels.

At the top of a short hill, past the college, the road bends right but the Way continues straight on into a field and then runs on the right-hand side of a fence. Over to the left is Aldershot and, closer

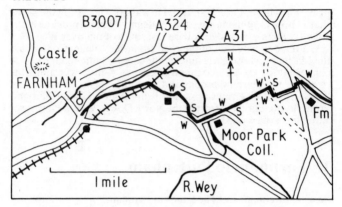

and downhill, some sandpits. At a beechwood turn right at the second stile into an old sunken trackway uphill. At a modern bungalow turn left down a path beside a private road and then, at Hunters Lodge, cross a road to a passage that leads into Sands Road.

The Way turns right along Sands Road and at a golf clubhouse turns left into Blighton Lane. Straight on, off the Way, is The Sands, a tiny collection of houses with a pub, post-office stores and church. Where Blighton Lane bends left the Way leaves it to run beside the golf course. Over to the right, and somewhat behind, is Crooksbury Hill, an unusual conical hill about 550 feet (170 m) high.

The Way crosses a road (Binton Lane) and at a fork keeps to the right of a small pine copse and then right of a hedge. The Hog's Back Hotel can be seen up on the ridge to the left. After crossing a track the path crosses a road which, to the left, runs down into Seale.

Seale is a small village with a number of renovated cottages. The church was built at the expense of Waverley Abbey just after 1200 but the present building is mostly Victorian. It is largely built of clunch, a form of hard chalk. A memorial in the north transept depicts the collision of two British ships on their way to Spain in 1809, erected by a schoolfellow of one of those who drowned.

After crossing the road the Way runs up beside a white house and then turns left to the other side of the ridge. The pine trees below hide the seventeenth-century East End Farm but there is a view along the south side of the Hog's Back. The Hog's Back is a 7-mile-long ridge of sand crowned with chalk that runs between Farnham and Guildford. The A31 along the ridge is a direct descendant of a track used since neolithic times and probably

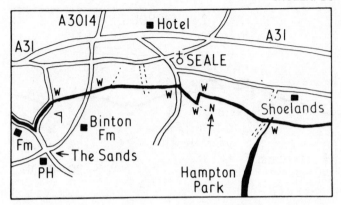

earlier. The name is generally taken to refer to the shape of the ridge but possibly is derived from the Celtic word *ogof* meaning giant.

The path turns right along the edge of the valley. Ahead, in the bottom of the valley, is Shoelands, a Tudor house. Its name may refer to the 'shoolers' or beggars, who preyed on pious travellers along the Pilgrim's Way.

The path leads down through some trees to cross the private drive of the Hampton Estate. It crosses a little stream that supplies a series of ponds and dams that provided water for Cutt Mill. A narrow path leaves the track to the left and climbs up to sandy Puttenham Common. To the left is the Hog's Back and to the right is the parallel greensand ridge. On the far side of the heath a narrow path runs down to the top of Lascombe Lane. The lane is followed downhill to join the road from Seale at the end of The Street in Puttenham.

The charming village of Puttenham used to have a pilgrims' fair, timed to coincide with the December festival of St Thomas. In the short walk to the church a number of old cottages are passed. The village pub, the Good Intent, has as its sign Cromwell praying in his tent. Just inside the churchyard gate is the old village well which was filled in during the mid 1700s and only came to light on Palm Sunday in 1972 because a cypress tree suddenly dropped several feet into it.

The church was started about 1160 and the tower is fifteenth-century. The spire was lost in a fire that started in the village blacksmith's in 1735. A brass on the chancel wall commemorates ninety-six years of consecutive office as rector of a father and son, both called Henry Beedell. The Palladian house behind the church, Puttenham Priory, was built in 1762. It was never part of a

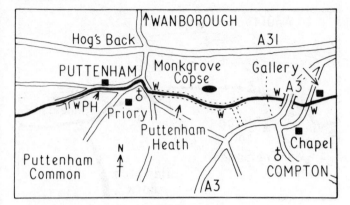

monastery but was so called because the manor was once the property of the Prior of Newark.

The Way continues between the church and the weatherboarded barns of Greys Home Farm and, by a wrought iron sign commemorating the Queen's silver jubilee, turns right towards the Jolly Farmers on the B3000.

2. Puttenham to Guildford

Buses: Puttenham and Compton to Guildford and Farnham.
Parking: opposite the Jolly Farmers at Puttenham; Watts Gallery and church at Compton.
Pubs: Jolly Farmers (restaurant) at Puttenham; Ship, close to St Catherine's Chapel.

The Way runs down the track opposite the Jolly Farmers and to the left of the golf club. This area, close to the Surrey-Hampshire border, was the nursery of modern cricket in the 1700s and the present pitch that is passed on the right can easily be imagined as a chosen site.

The track continues, passing Monkgrove Copse and Monk Grove Cottages. It ignores a track to the right, passes Questors and church at Compton. After crossing another path enters Hurt Hills Wood. The Way passes under a stone arch carrying the A3, which is marked on either side by wooden crosses, an unusual reminder that this is the old Pilgrims' Way. A little further on Down Lane is reached, opposite the Watts Gallery, Compton.

G. F. Watts (1817–1904) was a popular late Victorian painter and lived at the nearby house called Limnerlease. Watts's first wife was Ellen Terry but it was his second wife, Mary Fraser-Tyler, who

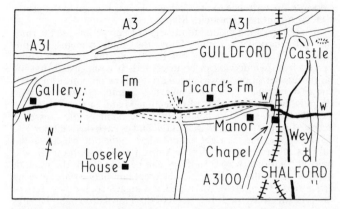

built the gallery. It is full of his mainly allegorical paintings as well as examples of his drawings and sculptures. She also built, using only local labour, the memorial chapel on a mound in the cemetery. Nothing about the terracotta exterior prepares one for the shock of the art nouveau and heavy symbolism of the highly decorated inside.

Compton church is notable for its unique double sanctuary that probably used to house a holy relic. The Norman wooden balustrade, made from a single plank, is one of the oldest pieces of wood used for its original purpose in England. Other treasures of the partly Saxon church include recently discovered mural patterns, a scratched figure of a twelfth-century knight, some very early stained glass and interesting brasses. In 1906 six skeletons on top of each other were discovered close to the foundations. They were probably the hermit occupants of the church's anchorite cells. A board below the window of the Norman cell, by the stairs to the upper altar, is worn thin where their hands rested in prayer.

Returning to the Way, it runs along the sandy track beside the Watts Gallery, passing some farm buildings, and into pleasant woodland. Opposite the eighteenth-century Conduit farmhouse a glimpse is caught of the back of Loseley House. It was built in the 1560s as the seat of the More family, using stone from Waverley Abbey, and boasts no less than three ghosts.

By the driveway to Conduit Farm, with a radio mast on a hill to the left, the track forks and the Way keeps left. It bears left into a field on the left and crosses to a stile in the far corner. After 50 yards it crosses a track and continues on to pass Picards Farm. In ¾ mile, beyond the farm, the Way turns left into Sandy Lane and runs down to the junction with the A3100.

At the Ship turn right and shortly left down Ferry Lane,

opposite the entrance to the College of Law, housed in the partly sixteenth-century Braboeuf Manor.

At the top of the mound to the right of Ferry Lane are the ruins of St Catherine's Chapel. Only the shell remains of this fourteenth-century building but five doors, the upper two converted from windows, can be discerned. It is suggested that the large number of doors was necessary to allow pilgrims to file past some holy relic. A legend says two giantesses built the twin chapels, St Martha's (passed in section 3) and St Catherine's, to expiate some sins, but having only one hammer they tossed it across the valley to each other at the end of each day's labour.

The chapel had the right to hold a fair on the hill, which was the subject of a picture by Turner. A much more important fair was held at Shalford, whose rooftops can be seen, from the mound, down in the valley to the right. The great fair, at one time covering 140 acres (57 hectares), was timed, it is suggested, for the return of the pilgrims from the July festival of the Translation of St Thomas in Canterbury. It may have given John Bunyan, who lived on Shalford Common at one time, the idea for Vanity Fair and the nearby marshy ground may be the inspiration for the Slough of Despond.

At the bottom of Ferry Lane a misleading sign declares this to be the path Chaucer's pilgrims trod. In fact they went from London straight to Canterbury. At the bottom of Friary Lane turn right along the towpath and cross the river over the footbridge. Turn left for 25 yards then turn right to go through Shalford Park.

Guildford

Tourist information: Civic Hall, London Road (telephone: Guildford 67314).

Buses: to Farnham, Woking, Dorking etc (telephone: Guildford 75735); coach services to London.

Trains: to Aldershot, Woking, London (Waterloo), Dorking (Deepdene) etc (telephone enquiries: Woking 65251).

Places of interest: Guildford House, open Monday to Saturday, 10.30–5; Museum, open Monday to Saturday 11–5; Castle, open daily April to September; Grammar School and Guildhall, open by prior arrangement only; Hospice, 11–12 and 3–4 Saturday only.

Guildford commands the narrow gap in the North Downs carved out by the river Wey. It was the ancient capital of Surrey and is now a busy shopping, commercial and educational centre.

The High Street, paved with granite setts, climbs up from the river. Most of the major buildings of interest lie on or close to it.

The street was declared the most beautiful in the kingdom by Dickens. An earlier writer, Defoe, drew attention to its attraction in having the town gallows so placed that townspeople could 'sit at their shop doors, and see criminals executed'.

Near the top of the High Street is the Royal Grammar School. The school was founded in 1507 and the present building completed in 1586. The chained library contains more than ninety rare old books.

The Hospital of the Holy Trinity was built as a hospice by George Abbot between 1619 and 1622. It includes a chapel, with fine stained glass windows, a refectory and banqueting chamber, all of which are open at certain times. Several seventeenth- and eighteenth-century Dutch paintings can be seen and a portrait that has been attributed to Hogarth. The blue coat that the occupants sometimes wear is made from a woollen cloth that was peculiar to the Guildford district in the middle ages.

The ornate Church of the Holy Trinity, on the opposite side of the High Street, is mid eighteenth-century and contains a monument to the hospice founder, Archbishop Abbot. His effigy lies under a highly decorated canopy and on top of carved stone columns of books and grills displaying mawkish skulls and bones. George Abbot was born in Guildford in 1562 and educated at the grammar school. While Archbishop of Canterbury he accidentally killed a keeper while shooting deer and spent the rest of his life believing himself a murderer. The church also contains a monument to Arthur Onslow, who was speaker of the House of Commons for thirty-three years in the 1700s, the third member of his family to hold the office.

A few yards down the High Street is Guildford House. It was built in 1660 for a merchant, John Child, with decorated plaster ceilings and a marvellous carved staircase. It is open throughout the year as an art exhibition centre.

This section of the High Street is dominated by the Guildhall clock. The case was made in 1683 but the original works of 1560 have been replaced with modern ones. The blue and white front of the Guildhall has been aptly likened to the poop of an old ship. Close by, the Angel Hotel is a reminder of when Guildford was a major posting station on the coach route to Portsmouth. The signs on the Georgian front boldly declare 'Posting house' and 'Livery stables'. Much of the rest of the building is seventeenth-century and the crypt, now a bistro, is a rare example of early fourteenth-century architecture. Another crypt, of similar age, lies below a building society office at 72 High Street and may shortly be open to visitors.

South of the High Street on the top of a mound, converted to public gardens, stands the hollow square keep that is the only substantial part of Guildford Castle still standing. There may have

15

been a castle here in Saxon times but the present structure was built by Henry II. It is built of Burgate stone and flint and incorporates fragments of Roman tiles. From the top of the castle mound there is an excellent view of the cathedral and university on Stag Hill.

The cathedral was begun in 1936 and was consecrated in 1961. It was the first Anglican cathedral to be built in the south of England since the Reformation. The design, by Sir Edward Maufe, makes the interior airy and spacious.

Below the castle, in Castle Hill, is The Chestnuts, where the sisters of Charles Dodgson, better known as Lewis Carroll, lived and it was the house where he died. A plaque commemorating his association with the house is decorated with characters from the two 'Alice' books.

At the corner of Castle Hill and Quarry Street, by an old gateway to the castle, stands Guildford Museum. It contains a good archaeological and geological collection, articles from the town's history and some fine old toys.

Guildford's oldest church, St Mary's, further down Quarry Street, has a Saxon tower which may not originally have been attached to the church. Other parts of the church were added between the eleventh and thirteenth centuries. The structure of the church changed dramatically in 1825 when 12 feet (3.7 m) behind the high altar were knocked down. This was done at the urging of the Prince Regent, who was unable to drive his coach and four through the narrow gap between the prison and church in Quarry Street on his way to Brighton. He is accused of having offered to pay but refusing to honour this pledge once the alterations were completed. Just inside the main door, on the west wall, is a curious low window; various suggestions have been made as to its purpose: that it was a lepers' window, to hear confessions, or to show a light to guide travellers over the ford. The north chapel (St John's) used to have a group of medieval frescoes but only a small section of pattern on the entrance arch survives.

At the bottom of the High Street is Friary Street. The Dominican friary founded by Queen Eleanor and the Friary Meux brewery that stood here have now both disappeared. The stained glass windows in the chapel of the hospice may have come from the friary.

On the other side of the river the mainly Victorian church of St Nicholas contains a Jacobean monument to Sir William More.

From the bottom of the High Street to the left, along Millbrook (A281) and past the Yvonne Arnaud Theatre, is the Jolly Farmer and the start of section 3.

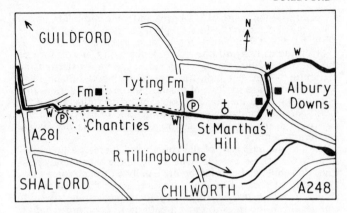

3. Guildford to Netley Heath

Buses: Chilworth and Albury to Guildford and Dorking.
Trains: Chilworth to Guildford and Dorking (Deepdene).
Parking: Guildford, car parks close to the Jolly Farmer and
   Chantry Cottage; Halfpenny Lane (near Tyting Farm); West
   Hanger; Newlands Corner.
Pubs: in Guildford including the Jolly Farmer (riverside patio,
   food).
Toilets: Newlands Corner.

The Way crosses from Shalford Park into Pilgrims' Way.
Where the road bends left the Way forks right and takes the
track to the left of Chantry Cottage, along the northern edge of
the wooded ridge called Chantries. The track is easily followed
for 1 mile until it turns left into Halfpenny Lane, the minor road
from Chilworth. It passes Tyting Farm, which had a twelfth - or
thirteenth-century oratory, probably the residence of the priest
in charge of St Martha's Chapel. The Way, however, turns right
about 15 yards up the road and then takes the wide path that
leads up to St Martha's Chapel.

St Martha's Hill was probably a site of pre-Christian worship
and some six hundred early Christians are said to have been
massacred here. The dedication of the chapel to St Martha is
unusual and may be a corruption of 'martyrs'. An unlikely legend
says the saint visited the spot with Joseph of Arimathea and
Lazarus. The Saxon and Norman chapel fell into ruin after the
dissolution of the monasteries and the present building dates
mainly from the mid nineteenth century. The church contains a

pleasant wooden figure of St Martha and some coffin lids, one of which may be that of Cardinal Stephen Langton, a representative of the barons at Runnymede for the signing of Magna Carta.

From the churchyard one can look down on Chilworth where the fall of the Tillingbourne was an ideal site for a watermill and made the village an industrial centre. Cobbett, about 1800, blamed the village for 'two of the most damnable inventions that ever sprang from the minds of man under the influences of the devil! Namely the making of gunpowder and of bank-notes!' An explosion at the gunpowder factory damaged St Martha's in the eighteenth century.

Next to the east gate of the churchyard there is a memorial stone to the actress Yvonne Arnaud. From the gate a sandy path leads downhill and bears left before a pillbox through some trees to Guildford Lane. The Way turns left along the road and in about ¼ mile turns right into a path through some trees. It emerges from the trees to cross a path on to open grassland on Albury Downs.

Below, to the right, is the village of Albury, which was moved by the squire of Albury Park, Henry Drummond, in the early nineteenth century from its site in the park to what was then called Weston Street. The church is based on one Drummond admired in Normandy.

The path leads up to Newlands Corner, probably after Box Hill the most popular beauty spot in Surrey. It is named after Abraham Newland, a signatory of some of the banknotes minted at Chilworth.

The Way crosses the road and continues along a bridlepath a little to the right of some tea rooms. Unfortunately there are no views but the woodland is very pleasant. Weston Wood, down the hill, is named after the one-time owners of Albury House.

Trackways like this were important smuggling routes in the days when the export of wool was taxed. Wool from Guildford was taken along the North Downs to Ranmore and down to the Dorking gap. Excise duty was gradually transferred to goods entering the country and smuggling flourished in the eighteenth century; specially constructed large cellars for contraband are still to be found in some houses in Shere.

The Way passes a footpath leading downhill to the chalk strata of the Downs where a spring head forms Silent Pool. Martin Tupper, a resident of Albury, in his romantic novel *Stephen Langton*, publicised a legend associated with it. The pool is supposedly haunted by the ghost of a local forester's daughter. While bathing she was surprised by Prince John and in her attempt to escape fell into the deep water and was drowned.

1½ miles from Newlands Corner the Way crosses Staple Lane at West Hanger; 200 yards on it crosses a second road into the drive

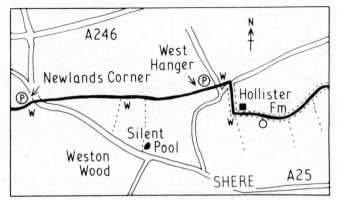

of Hollister Farm and then turns left along a concrete track through the trees. A footpath to the right of the farm leads to Shere, which has the reputation of being the prettiest village in Surrey.

The Way passes a concrete water reservoir and continues for 1¼ miles to another reservoir on Netley Heath above Colekitchen Farm.

4. Netley Heath to Boxlands

Buses: from the villages along the A25 to Dorking or Guildford; Ranmore Common to Dorking.
Trains: Gomshall to Dorking (Deepdene).
Parking: Ranmore Common.

There is no access by road to the start of this section but a footpath runs up to the way from Colekitchen Lane in Gomshall. A leather factory in Gomshall claims to be the most ancient leatherworks in Britain, dating from before the Domesday survey.

The Way continues along the ridge on Netley Heath, named after the abbey in Hampshire which owned the manor in the thirteenth century. The previous owner, Peter de Manley, may have executed Prince Arthur, who had stood between King John and the throne.

In about 1/3 mile on Hackhurst Downs, by an overgrown concrete reservoir, the Way forks downhill to the right. As it descends it keeps to the left, passing through some trees on to a grassy slope. At the other end of this open area a path continues along the side of the Downs.

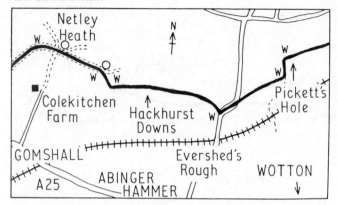

The village of Abinger Hammer, below, takes its name not from the well known clock that has 'Jack the Smith' striking the hour but from the hammer ponds on the Tillingbourne. The ponds were used to power the hammers of the local iron foundries that have now disappeared. Nowadays they are used for watercress beds and fish farming.

The path passes several pillboxes. In the last war the Downs here were an important munitions dump. About 1¼ miles from the fork the path bends down by a pillbox to the minor road that runs from the A25 to Effingham (White Down Lane). Crossways Farm at the junction with the A25 must have been known to George Meredith, who lived at Box Hill and wrote the novel *Diana of the Crossways*. Evershed's Rough, just south of the railway, was where the out-spoken Bishop Samuel Wilberforce was killed by a fall from his horse in 1873. He was known as Soapy-Sam because he was always getting into hot water.

The Way turns left up the road but in a few yards leaves it to the right, to run along the side of the White Downs. Below lies the partly Norman church of Wotton. It contains memorials to the Evelyn family, who lived, from the sixteenth to the twentieth century, at Wotton House, set among the trees to the right of the Wotton Hatch Inn on the A25. John Evelyn, the diarist, was born and died in the house. Today it is a fire service college.

The Way climbs up to enter some trees, by a pillbox, and runs above Pickett's Hole, the valley of a dried-up spring. The line of the Way along the ridge of the Downs is occasionally marked by paint on the trees. At the point where it crosses the second bridleway there is a good view of Westcott, a tidy village that straddles the A25. It was the birthplace in 1766 of Thomas Malthus, who prophesied that population growth would increase

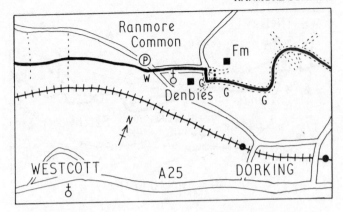

faster than the means of subsistence until checked by famine and disease.

From the bridlepath a path runs to Ranmore Common, where the Way crosses the road to run past Ranmore church. It was built in 1859 to a design by Sir Gilbert Scott at the expense of Lord Ashcombe, the son of Thomas Cubitt. Cubitt started as a carpenter but founded a business that built large parts of Belgravia and he died a millionaire. A little further on the road passes Denbies, where most of the great house Cubitt built for himself in 1850 has disappeared.

At North Lodge the Way turns right off the road and then, after 50 yards, turns left down the old Denbies drive, passing through a vineyard. (A diversion application may slightly alter this short section of the route). In the eighteenth century the estate was owned by Jonathon Tyers, the founder of the Vauxhall Gardens. In contrast to the pleasure gardens, the eccentric Tyers set out the grounds here to be as gloomy as possible, with a temple covered in sad texts, pictures of a Christian and an unbeliever in their dying agonies, pedestals topped by human skulls and a clock that struck every minute to remind people of approaching death.

The drive winds round the hill, crosses a track, then forks right downhill, through some rhododendrons. It flattens out and passes under the railway. Camilla Lacey, ¼ mile to the left, was the house Fanny Burney bought from the proceeds of her novel *Camilla*.

The Way crosses the A24 by a subway a little way to the left. Past the the subway is the Burford Bridge Hotel, previously called the Fox and Hounds. Nelson made his farewell to Lady Hamilton at the hotel before leaving for the Battle of Trafalgar.

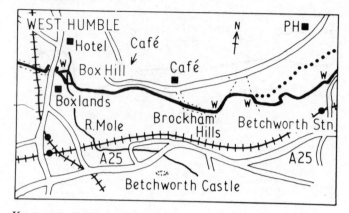

Keats stayed there and claimed that a walk on Box Hill by moonlight gave him the inspiration for part of *Endymion*.

Dorking, a mile to the right, is an ancient market town and, nowadays, a prosperous commuter centre. The spire of St Martin's, which is clearly seen from Ranmore and Box Hill, is a memorial to Bishop Wilberforce.

5. Boxlands to Wingate Hill

Buses: along A 24 to Dorking or Leatherhead; Box Hill to Leatherhead.

Trains: from Dorking (North) or Boxhill and Westhumble to Leatherhead and London (Victoria or Waterloo) or Horsham; Dorking (Deepdene) and Betchworth to Guildford or Reigate.

Parking: by the stepping stones or Burford Bridge Hotel; top of Box Hill.

From the subway under the A24 the Way turns right but shortly turns left down a track to the stepping stones across the river Mole. The river downstream is notable in dry periods for disappearing down swallow holes and running underground. About 1700 an improbable experiment where a duck was forced down a swallow hole and reappeared downstream with all its feathers rubbed off was reported. The apt name of Mole in its earliest form (Mulesey) only meant the land abutting the water belonging to someone called Mul.

The river can either be crossed by the hexagonal stones, donated by Mr Ede (one-time Home Secretary), or by the foot-bridge a few yards away. The path continues uphill, passing between a few box trees, which gave their name to the hill. John

22

Aubrey, writing in 1718, mentioned that the 'great quantity and thickness of the box wood yielded convenient privacy for lovers, who frequently meet here'. The owner of the hill in 1800 sold large numbers of trees for felling but, fortunately for later generations of lovers, the glut caused the price to fall so the rest were saved.

The path climbs steeply, through yew trees, with its line marked by paint on trees. It comes out at the top of Box Hill a few yards away from an observation point and seat. The path from the Burford Bridge Hotel comes up the other side of Swiss Cottage, near the popular Fort Café. Not far down this path is the grave of Major Peter Labelliere, an eighteenth-century Dorking eccentric. At his own request he was buried head downwards and one of his landlady's children danced on his grave.

The Way runs below the road along the hill, passing just below another café. About ¾ mile from the observation point, by a plantation, it bends left and then turns right along a track. At the hairpin bend descend the steps and steep slope and turn left along the path above the chalk pit. The pits here may be very old in origin, early man digging for flints and the Romans quarrying the chalk for road foundations and for lime to make a hard cement.

At the fork keep right, below the caravan site, and at the pathway, by Quick's grave, turn right downhill. The designated route will keep straight on here but at the moment the path leads down and round the lower edge of the Betchworth Pit, through the arches of one of the brick bridges. It comes out at a row of houses and on to Pebblehill Road, Betchworth, by the entrance to Holmes Farm. The Way turns left up the road but soon after a left bend leaves it to the east through a strip of trees. After ¼ mile it turns left, through a gate, up to the trees. At the trees, by a pylon, it takes the right fork.

Below, the houses of Buckland can just be seen. In 1725 a rector dismissed Buckland as having 'no chapel, no curate, no papists, no non-conformists, no school'. The name does not refer to deer but is a corruption of Bokland or Bookland, meaning land exchanged by delivery of a book (or deed).

The Way joins another path but leaves it to the left, just past a chalk pit, and so keeps above the fields. At the end of a field a path forking right, down to Underhill Farm, is ignored. At the bridle-path, barred off from the footpath, the Way turns left up Colley Hill. The bridlepath is followed to the top, where it comes out by The Swiss House, the other side of which a path is followed to the escarpment of Colley Hill.

The Way continues along a gravel path but every walker will leave it a few yards to the right to enjoy the view above Reigate from the grassy slopes. The slopes have the descriptive names of Saddle Knob and the Horseshoe and are favourite sites for those flying model gliders.

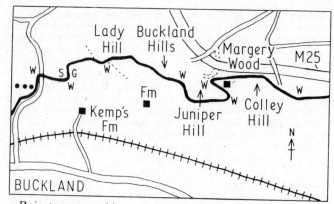

Reigate was an old market town but is now another dormitory area for London. It was an important coaching staging post but suffered a decline in the early days of the railway because the line went through Redhill to the east. In the main street, causing an obstruction to traffic, is the brick town hall built in 1728.

The Way passes a water tower and the edge of Margery Wood. By a folly containing a broken drinking fountain it starts along a broad track. This track is followed for ¾ mile, crossing another track on the way, to the footbridge over the A217 and the car park on Wingate Hill.

6. Wingate Hill to War Coppice Garden Village

Buses: Wingate Hill (A217) to Reigate, Epsom or Sutton; Merstham to Reigate, Redhill or Croydon.
Trains: Merstham to Redhill or Croydon and London (Victoria or London Bridge).
Parking: Wingate Hill; on road mainly at Merstham.
Pubs: Feathers (food, garden) and others in Merstham; Harrow (food, garden, children's room), Stanstead Road.
Toilets: Wingate Hill and Merstham.

On the far side of the car park at Wingate Hill from the foot-bridge the Way enters Gatton Park. The major path is followed, somewhat downhill initially, for ½ mile to the drive of the Royal Alexandra and Albert School. The Way turns right down the drive

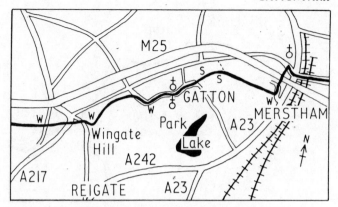

and passes the school houses and then the school chapel.

To the right of the Way at the chapel is Gatton church, which contains woodwork treasures from all over Europe collected by Lord Monson, the owner of the park in the 1830s. The church key may be obtained on enquiry from a house close to the park.

Gatton Park was described by Cobbett as a 'very rascally spot of earth' because it was a 'rotten borough', sending two members to Parliament even though the electorate was often only the owner. In 1542 the owner elected himself both members. Past some classrooms, to the right of the church, is the smallest town hall in Britain, a classical folly, in the form of a little temple, of 1765.

At the school chapel the Way turns left and leaves the park by the North Lodge. It turns right down Rocky Lane but shortly leaves it to the left down a private road behind the Dower House. This leads into a path along the side of a field with the M25 over to the left. The Way keeps to the right and after ¾ mile comes up past a cricket ground into Quality Street, Merstham.

The name Quality Street is the result of a joke that stuck. Seymour Hicks and Ellanine Terris lived in the fifteenth-century Old Forge House, at the end of the street, while appearing in Barrie's play of that name.

Merstham owed its importance to its position in a gap in the North Downs and to the quarrying of stone, some of which was used for the first London Bridge and Westminster Palace. In 1805 it was connected to the first railway in the world – a line of hoppers pulled by horses. The rails were flanged, not the wheels, so the trucks could run on roads if necessary.

The Way turns left along Quality Street and then right along a footpath beside the Old Forge. It crosses the M25 by a footbridge to a road just below St Katherine's. The church contains clappers

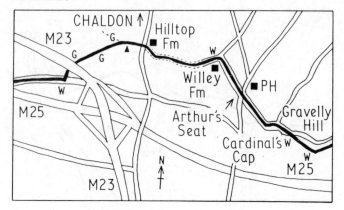

from the old bells and a battered stone figure of a mayor of London five hundred years ago, which was discovered face down being used as a paving stone.

Turn right along the road and cross the A23 into Rockshaw Road opposite. To the right, by the station, is an LCC overspill estate of the 1950s. After ½ mile turn down a path to the left, just before some bungalows, which leads down to a subway under the M23. On the other side the Way climbs diagonally uphill, passes through some trees and continues on until it reaches a gate at the top.

Below, to the right of the M23, fuller's earth quarries can be seen near Nutfield. Fuller's earth has been used since Roman times for washing greasy materials and more recently in the manufacture of soaps and pigments and as an industrial filter medium. Bletchingley, to the left of the motorway, had a castle, of which little remains, and was the manor given to Anne of Clèves by Henry VIII after their divorce.

The Way runs east along the top of the ridge and passes a triangulation point (662 feet or 202 metres). It crosses Hilltop Lane, which to the north runs into Chaldon. Chaldon church, a mile to the north of the Way, is renowned for a large thirteenth-century wall painting. The track signposted to Roverdene is followed. It passes the Caterham District Scout Camp and ¾ mile from the road reaches Willey Farm. Just past the farm on the right is a curious little folly. Keeping right, follow the farm drive out to Stanstead Road.

The Way crosses into War Coppice Road opposite to pass Arthur's Seat, a possible site of an iron-age fort. On the left is the stone Whitehill Tower. In about ¼ mile the road passes the entrance to The Mound, a house built on the site of an earthworks called Cardinals Cap. The collection of expensive houses here is War Coppice Garden Village. 'War' may be derived from an old Norse word meaning a beacon.

7. War Coppice Garden Village to Betsoms Hill Farm

Buses: along A22 to Godstone or Caterham; The Ridge (north of South Hawke) to Woldingham or Caterham; Chalkpit Lane (from south of the Way) to Oxted; Botley Hill to Sanderstead and Croydon or Westerham or Oxted.
Trains: Oxted to Croydon and London (Victoria).
Parking: mainly on road, a little at Gravelly Hill.

The Way runs along War Coppice Road and then, at Hextalls Lane, leaves it to the right along a path below the summit of Gravelly Hill. After ½ mile the path rejoins the road by a grassy area with a panoramic view to the south. The road passes a water tap and, in about 100 yards, the Way leaves it again to the right along a track below an earthworks (Pilgrims' Fort Camp). The track leads round the hill, crossing another path, and then by a small caravan park joins a minor road to Caterham (Tupwood Lane). Turn right but after a few yards, where the road bends left, keep straight on over the bridge crossing the A22. On the other side cross a field, then turn right into a track, part of the Roman road that ran through Godstone, but after a few yards bear left over a stile. The path winds round to come out in front of some warehouses, at the disused Godstone quarries. Cross the road into a path above Quarry Cottage and climb up to the track past Winders Hill Cottages.

Marden Castle, a shooting lodge, is hidden to the left in trees. The track comes out at South Lodge by the entrance to Marden Park, now the Convent of the Sacred Heart, a Roman Catholic school for girls. The village of Marden was wiped out by the Black Death in 1348–9. In the mid seventeenth century Sir Robert Clayton, a wealthy London merchant, built a house in the park. That house was destroyed by fire in 1879 and was replaced by one of Victorian Gothic. The park was the home of William Wilberforce when he was working on his crusade to free slaves.

The Way continues over a stile into a path leading uphill to some trees. After 200 yards it takes a right fork down to Gangers Hill (a continuation of Flower Lane), which it crosses to a path through Hanging Wood to another road. The Way turns left, beside the road, until it rejoins Gangers Hill. It runs just below the road to

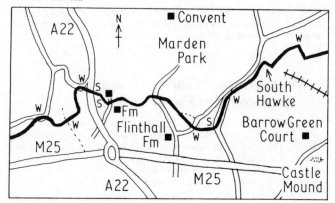

some seats at South Hawke, overlooking Oxted and Limpsfield. Down to the right is Barrow Green Court, the seventeenth-century manor house of Oxted. At the beginning of the nineteenth century it was the home of Jeremy Bentham, the radical political thinker. The Castle Mound, covered in trees, behind the house is said to be a prehistoric fortification but it may be a natural feature.

Oxted (*Ac stede* – the place of oak trees) is an old village with some sixteenth-century buildings. A newer part has grown up round the station. Limpsfield, between the A25 and the line of the new motorway (M25), has some fifteenth- and sixteenth-century brick and timber houses. Delius, the composer, is buried in the churchyard.

Just past the seats at South Hawke the Way turns right, away from the road, down some steps above Oxted railway tunnel. The tunnel was built in 1878 and was a considerable engineering feat. The path turns left along the hillside and in about ¼ mile turns right down a not very obvious path and then left to run below the trees that surround a large quarry pit. At the road (Chalkpit Lane) that has come up from Oxted under the motorway cross on to a path a little way down to the right. This path climbs to the top of a rise and then runs along the edge of the Titsey Plantation. The red brick building with a spire on the hill over to the right dates from 1886 and is a girls' school.

After about ½ mile the Way turns left into a track that climbs uphill. It passes a gate on the right which allows a rare view of Titsey Place below. The house was built in 1775 for Sir John Gresham but altered in the 1830s. Sir John had the church of St James, which stood close to the house, removed to where it stands in the village. South of the house the remains of a Roman villa, which seems to have been used for the fulling of cloth, were

28

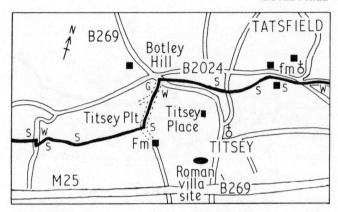

discovered in 1867.

The track climbs up to the top of Botley Hill, previously called Coldharbour Green. It is the highest point (874 feet or 265 metres) on the North Downs but is, unfortunately, surrounded by trees. Turn right into a path that runs to the left of the road to Titsey (B269). After ½ mile turn left uphill and then right, above a field, to a narrow road and cross into a wood. Out of the trees, climb diagonally up to the B2024 and turn right along the path below the road. After ¼ mile cross the road into Hill Park. A little way up the road to the left is the charming little Norman church of Tatsfield, isolated from the village: this is one of the highest churches in Britain.

The Way runs along the road through Hill Park and in about ½ mile takes the fork to the right. A little way down a white gate marks the Surrey-Kent border. The road runs on down to the A233. Betsoms Hill Farm is a short distance down to the right but the Way crosses straight over the main road.

8. Betsoms Hill Farm to Otford

Buses: along A233 to Biggin Hill or Westerham; Knockholt to Orpington or Sevenoaks; Dunton Green to Sevenoaks.
Trains: Dunton Green to Sevenoaks or Orpington and London (Charing Cross).
Parking: on roads only.
Pubs: Tally-Ho (garden) and Crown at Knockholt; Harrow and Three Horseshoes at Knockholt Pound (north of Chevening Park); Rose and Crown at Dunton Green.

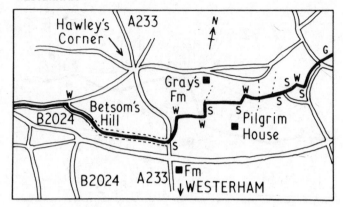

From the private road the Way has followed, cross the A233 to the path opposite. To the right the A233 runs down to Westerham, an ancient country town. One of the old houses was used by William Pitt as a country retreat. The town was the birthplace of General James Wolfe and he lived at Quebec House, now owned by the National Trust. There are statues of Wolfe and also Churchill, who lived at Chartwell 2½ miles to the south, on the green.

The path climbs uphill, then bends right below a quarry and through some yew trees. It runs above a field and then left up some steps through trees and up the hill. At the junction with another path it turns right to run above Pilgrim House. After 500 yards keep left to go round a field. At the top keep right and go along through some oak trees and in about ½ mile turn right down towards the road running up Hogtrough Hill to Brasted. The path runs beside the road and keeps straight on at a T junction to run along a field's edge to the road by Stoneings Farm. Up the road ½ mile to the left is the Tally-Ho but the Way keeps straight on beside the road to Knockholt. In about 600 yards, where the road bends left it keeps straight on. At a gateway it turns left and then shortly right to a road, which it runs beside for about 100 yards and then turns right into a footpath on the other side of it.

Ahead, the road continues to come out in Knockholt, close to the church and the Crown. The little church of St Katherine dates from 1218.

The Way goes up the path to a stile at the edge of Chevening Park, keeps right round a cricket pitch, goes through a gap between some trees by a few derelict brick buildings and then turns right round the edge of several fields. From one of the stiles that are crossed there is an unusual view of Chevening House

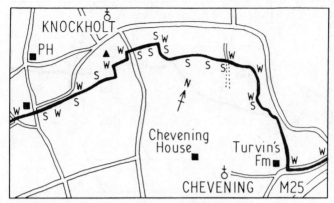

through a gap in the trees known as the Keyhole.

The main part of Chevening House was built in the early 1600s to a design by Inigo Jones. It belonged to the Earls of Stanhope from 1717 to 1967, when it was left to the nation. After being used for a short time by the then Lord Chancellor, Lord Hailsham, and then by the Prince of Wales, it became the official country residence of the Foreign Secretary.

The Way continues to an entrance to Chevening Park, where it goes into a path a few yards to the right. The path runs along the edge of a field and then continues between some trees into a field with a minor road from Knockholt Pound beside it. The Way keeps to the right and goes over an iron fence and turns left downhill towards Turvin's Farm.

Over to the right Chevening House and the church of St Botulph can be seen. The church dates from the thirteenth century and is unusual in shape, the nave being shorter than the south aisle. The church stood on the old road which carried the fish packhorses from Rye to London.

At the B2211 the Way turns left and then right into the A2028 across the A21. The road (Morants Court Road) in about ½ mile reaches a road junction by the Rose and Crown. Turn left and then right into the footpath behind the car park of the Donnington Manor Restaurant. In about ½ mile the path crosses a railway bridge and then follows a track past an orchard into Telston Lane. At the bottom of Telston Lane the Way turns right into Pilgrims' Way West and over the river Darent into Otford.

The road runs through Otford past Boughton Manor, a partly Tudor building, and Pickmoss, a timbered house built in the fourteenth and fifteenth centuries. Further on the road reaches the village pond, which now functions as an unusual roundabout.

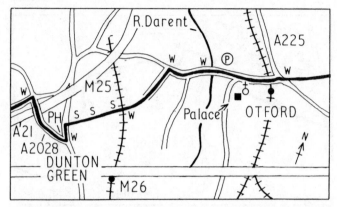

On the right is the partly Saxon church and behind it the shell of a Tudor palace that belonged to the Archbishops of Canterbury. Henry VIII stayed here on his way to the Field of the Cloth of Gold with a retinue of over four thousand. East of the palace is a spring that Archbishop Becket is said to have brought into being by striking the ground with his staff.

9. Otford to Wrotham

Buses: Otford to Sevenoaks or Kemsing; Wrotham to Borough Green.
Trains: Otford and Borough Green to London (Victoria) and Maidstone.
Parking: Otford; a little at crossing of minor road 1 mile from Wrotham.
Pubs: in Otford; Rising Sun (garden).
Toilets: Otford.

The Way runs up past Otford railway station and turns right off the A225 into Pilgrims' Way, signposted to Kemsing. After 50 yards it turns left, by The Mount, up a narrow path which climbs steeply uphill, with a view down on Otford behind, and passes a tumulus on the right. It runs beside a meadow and about a mile from The Mount reaches a road junction where it goes along the road opposite the stile for about 70 yards, then turns left into a field. A path runs round the edge of two fields then turns right into the drive of Hildenborough Hall, now a Christian conference centre. By the gates of the Hall the Way crosses a

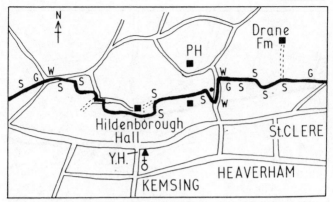

stile into a narrow path round the edge of a field. It drops down
to the right and then runs to the left along White Leaf Down,
land in the care of the Kent Trust for Nature Conservation.

The Way keeps left where the footpath forks downhill to
Kemsing, where the converted vicarage is now a youth hostel.
The Church of St Mary, below the hostel, has a shingled tower
and contains some attractive stained glass. A spring at the
crossroads is known as St Edith's Well and was reputed to have
the property of curing sore eyes. St Edith, the daughter of King
Edgar, was born in Kemsing in 961. For years afterwards grain
was brought to her shrine (destroyed in the Reformation) to be
blessed and ensure a good harvest.

On the Downs above Kemsing the Way crosses a path below
Hildenborough Hall. To the right a wooden cross has been
erected to overlook the valley. Past the walled gardens of the
Hall the Way turns left into a field and crosses somewhat back on
itself to a stile on the other side. It crosses another stile and turns
right to run beside a track for 50 yards and straight on through a
field. On the other side of a small wood the Way goes halfway
along a field and then crosses a stile into a drive to Kester. Turn
left uphill on the road and after ¼ mile turn right beside
Highfield Farm. Continue straight on past the farm and into a
path through a wood. On the far side the path runs under some
oak trees and then crosses a track and a stile to run along the
edge of a field. It goes through some trees and drops down to the
right to a road coming up from St Clere, a seventeenth-century
house.

The Way crosses the road to a path, a few yards to the right,
and then descends to another road. The surfaced road bends
right here but the Way turns left along the unsurfaced Pilgrims'

33

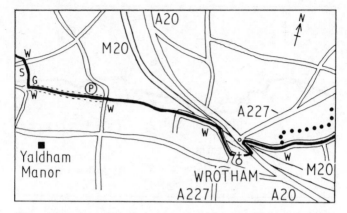

Way. After about ¾ mile it crosses another road into a path that runs beside an orchard. The path leads into Pilgrims' Way on the outskirts of Wrotham and continues on, passing tennis courts, and then takes a path leading up to the A20.

A little way down the road to the right is the centre of Wrotham and the parish church of St George. The church's west tower is pierced by an arch that was built to allow the Sunday morning procession to circle the church without leaving sacred ground. Crosses carved in the arch's stonework have been attributed to Canterbury pilgrims. Above the church porch is a figure of St George, a replacement, by the Royal Academy of Arts, for one stolen in 1971. The church contains some interesting brasses and a nuns' gallery. There used to be an archbishop's palace beside the church and behind where the Bull now stands.

10. Wrotham to Holly Hill

Buses: Wrotham to Maidstone and Gravesend.
Trains: Borough Green to London (Victoria) and Maidstone.
Parking: Wrotham; near the Vigo.
Pubs: Vigo; George at Trottiscliffe (food).

To return to the Way, cross the A20, turn left over the bridge crossing the M20, and at the junction with the A227 take the narrow road, Pilgrims' Way, off to the right. The Way continues along the road for about ½ mile and reaches a section where rights have not been negotiated and takes an alternative route. Continue straight ahead along the road and shortly the Way proceeds, by a series of stiles, along the line of Pilgrims' Way,

34

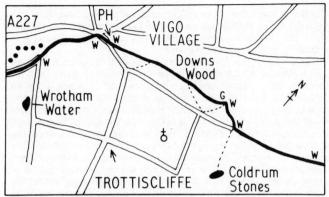

partly in the fields and partly on the road, passing Nepicar Lane to the right. In ¾ mile where Wrotham Water Road turns sharp right continue straight ahead along a track. In 50 yards the Way leaves to the left on a path which climbs steeply uphill through the wood and in 250 yards rejoins the designated Way. The path continues through the woods, passing the remains of a walled garden, and just past the wall to the right is a curious sunken circular brick chamber which is possibly the remains of an icehouse. Popular in the eighteenth and nineteenth centuries before the days of refrigeration, icehouses were constructed with a circular chamber below ground level, usually on a hill to facilitate drainage, and were roofed with straw or earth as insulation. The ice, usually from a nearby pond, was stored in the chamber between layers of straw and if well packed and salted would last for up to two years.

Continuing on, the path runs past a large brick gateway with wrought iron gates, which were once the entrance to Trosley Towers, which burned down in the 1930s. This was the home of Sir Sydney Waterlow, who was one of the founders of the Waterlow printing company. Opposite the gates is a small house which must have been the gatehouse. The Way runs along a wide track and in 300 yards joins the A227 for a short distance, then turns right down the road at the side of the Vigo. The inn once belonged to a sailor who fought with Admiral Rooke at Vigo Bay in 1702 and spent his prize-money on the pub.

The Way runs down the road for 200 yards, then turns left and enters the woods, passing through two barriers. The road continues steeply downhill to the remote village of Trottiscliffe. Actually pronounced and sometimes nowadays spelt 'Trosley', this is a delightful village set at the foot of the Downs in lovely countryside. There are some attractive inns and houses, one of

35

which was once the home of Graham Sutherland, and there is a good Norman church set somewhat remotely from the village. Inside the church is a carved pulpit with sounding board which was originally in Westminster Abbey.

Returning to the Way, it continues along a broad path through Downs Wood, which now forms part of Trosley Country Park. In about ¼ mile, ignore some earth steps with an arrow pointing downhill to the right and continue straight ahead following the path until it reaches a gate leading on to a bridlepath. Turn right along the path, which can be muddy, and continue downhill, past some houses, to the Pilgrims' Way and then turn left along the narrow path. Just to the right of this junction is a footpath leading across the fields to Coldrum Stones, a neolithic long barrow dating from at least 2000 BC. The great sarsen stones of the central burial chamber are in more or less their original position and round the mound are the fallen uprights of a stone circle. The site has been extensively excavated and the remains of a least twenty neolithic people found; this has led to the suggestion that Coldrum was a royal burial chamber. Some of the bones are on display in nearby Trottiscliffe church.

Returning to the Way, the path continues inside the edge of the wood at the foot of the Downs. In 1¼ miles, at a junction with a path leading to Birling Place Farm, turn left over a stile, cross a field and another stile and turn right along the edge of the fence. In 200 yards the path climbs steeply up the open Down and at the top there are superb views over the Medway valley. This is a popular place, particularly with picnickers in summer.

The Way leaves the Downs, crosses the road, continues along a road straight ahead past Holly Hill Lodge and in ½ mile arrives at the car park at Holly Hill.

11. Holly Hill to Borstal

Buses: Cuxton to Rochester; Borstal to Rochester.
Trains: Cuxton to Strood, Maidstone and London (Charing Cross).
Parking: car park at Holly Hill; and parking in Cuxton and Borstal.
Pubs: White Horse at Borstal; also in Cuxton.

From Holly Hill car park continue along the road towards Holly Hill Farm. About 50 yards past the farm the road ends and the Way joins a footpath that runs to the right along the edge of a plantation. In about 300 yards bear left through the plantation, to the right of which are a mass of rhododendrons, and shortly enter

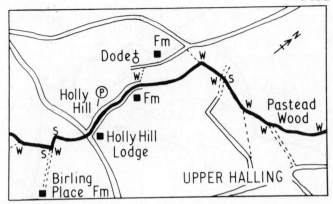

the main wood and continue along just inside the edge of it. The ridge slopes steeply away to the left and through the trees are occasional glimpses of the farm at Great Buckland in the valley.

Near the farm is the deserted Norman church of Dode. The village of Dode was decimated by plague in the years of the Black Death, leaving the church isolated and unused. Restored in the 1920s, the church still has only the farm near it but is occasionally used for special services.

At the edge of the wood turn right, go diagonally across a field and on the other side cross a farm road and continue through the edge of Horseholders Wood for 150 yards. The path then crosses a stile into a field and on the other side enters a wood which is mainly silver birch. Leaving this wood, cross another field, enter Pastead Wood and in about 400 yards cross a wide trackway which, to the right, leads down to Upper Halling.

An unlovely place, scarred by the cement works which lie along the river, Upper Halling achieved fame in 1912 when human bones believed to be twenty-five thousand years old were discovered and named 'Halling Man'. In the 1960s, however, modern dating techniques proved the bones to be neolithic and no more than four thousand years old. They are now in the Natural History Museum at Kensington.

Across the trackway the path continues through the wood and extensive felling has provided convenient resting places in the shape of tree stumps. Continuing on, the ridge falls sharply away on both sides of the path, giving good views. Shortly, turn left and descend steeply down the hillside, cross two stiles into a field and enter North Wood on the other side.

The Way goes through the wood, passing a large beech tree, and on the other side crosses a stile into a field. The path runs to the

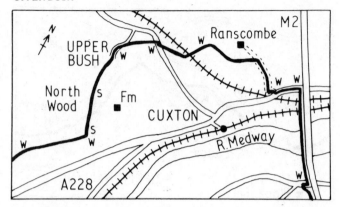

right diagonally down the valley and between the four attractive buildings that make up the tiny hamlet of Upper Bush. Past the houses, continue along a road for about 200 yards, then turn right diagonally across a field and then turn right along the road leading to Cuxton. In about 50 yards the Way turns left at the side of a house named Plovers and runs steeply up the hill on a path between the rear gardens of houses and a wood.

Continuing up the hill, the path crosses a railway line by a footbridge, then crosses a field and climbs steeply uphill. At the top of the hill the path runs to the right along the edge of the field and there are good views across the Medway valley. Turn left through a small spinney and continue on the other side along the edge of a field and in about 300 yards turn right along a farm track. Follow the track downhill until it joins the A228, cross the road, turn left along the footpath and in about 100 yards turn right across the Medway Bridge by the pedestrian way.

The bridge was built to carry the M2 motorway and rises on slender stilts over 100 feet (30 metres) above the river. There are spectacular views, to the right over the river valley and Wouldham Common and to the left down stream to Rochester Castle and Cathedral. Ahead, at the foot of the bridge lies the village of Borstal, which has given its name to Her Majesty's Institution for young offenders. The original, and still used, buildings can be seen on the hillside above. To the left of these is Borstal Fort; looking somewhat like an old earthworks, it was erected during the Napoleonic Wars as one of a chain of defences built along the Medway.

To the left of Borstal, on the water's edge, is a long slipway. Now used as a factory car park, it once belonged to Short Brothers Aviation and it was here that they built and launched their flying boats until 1946, when they moved their factories to Belfast.

Continuing across the river the path descends from the bridge and comes to the road which leads to the left into Borstal village and, further on, the centre of Rochester.

Rochester

Tourist information centre: 85 High Street (telephone: Medway 43666), open September to June, Monday to Saturday, July to August, every day.
Trains: frequent services to London and Kent coast; for information telephone West Malling 842842.
Buses: services to most parts of Kent and to London; telephone Medway 405251.
Places of interest: Guildhall Museum, High Street, open every day 12.30–5; Castle, Esplanade, open all year except Good Friday and Christmas Day (Sundays, afternoons only); Eastgate House (Dickens Centre), High Street, open every day 12.30–5.

Rochester lies on the south bank of the Medway and, although forming part of the urban sprawl known as the Medway Towns, it still manages to retain its own character.

The Romans founded their walled city of Durobrivae here on the site of a much older settlement; traces of the original walls can be found and a number of the buildings are over Roman foundations and vaults. The city is dominated by the massive Norman keep and by the cathedral, which lie close to the river, and the city has spread outwards from them.

The castle and cathedral were originally built by Bishop Gundulph between 1080 and 1100 but little remains of his original work. The massive keep, rising to 125 feet (38 metres), was added about a hundred years later and is one of the finest examples surviving in Britain. In 1215 King John besieged rebellious barons in the castle and undermined the south-east tower, causing part of it to crack and fall. It was subsequently restored with the militarily stronger round tower and inside the castle the repaired crack can be clearly seen. The inner wooden floors have disappeared but the stone staircases and galleries within the outer walls can still be climbed. Samuel Pepys once climbed to the top of the castle and was 'much afrighted by the precipice'. For braver souls, however, it offers superb views and from here is perhaps the best view of the cathedral and its magnificent west front.

Although one of Britain's smaller cathedrals, Rochester is still very fine in its detail. Part of Gundulph's original building remains in the north tower but the main building now dates from the late twelfth and early thirteenth centuries and has a Norman nave and

Early English choir. The west front is superb and the doorway a very fine example of Norman work, the only remaining example of a column figure doorway in England. Inside the cathedral, the vaulted undercroft still retains sections of Gundulph's original building; the best fourteenth-century work is the chapter-house doorway, dating from 1340. Much of the rebuilding work was paid for by offerings at the tomb of St William of Perth. A philanthropic baker, William was robbed and murdered outside Rochester whilst on a pilgrimage to Canterbury. The monks, seeing an opportunity to cream off some of the rich offerings from pilgrims on their way to Canterbury, quickly took the opportunity of canonising him and erecting a shrine.

Close by the cathedral is the old gateway known locally as either College Gate, Chertsey's Gate or Jasper's Gate, the last from its use by Charles Dickens as the residence of the sinister Jasper in *Edwin Drood*. As a boy Dickens lived in neighbouring Chatham and he returned to Rochester in later life and lived the last fifteen years of his life at nearby Gad's Hill. He used many of the buildings in Rochester as settings in his novels.

Rochester has solved most of its chronic traffic problems and a walk along the High Street, and its surrounding area, is a rewarding experience.

Near the bridge lies the Guildhall, built in 1687 and now used as the city museum, and opposite is the Royal Victoria and Bull Hotel, an eighteenth-century coaching inn originally known simply as the Bull until patronised by royalty in the 1800s! Further along, a large clock juts out over the street from the front of the Corn Exchange. The clock was a gift in 1706 from Admiral Sir Cloudsley Shovel, a former MP for Rochester, whose shipwrecked treasures in the Scilly Isles have, of recent years, been exciting archaeologists and skin-divers.

Beyond College Gate the buildings are cut away and another fine view of the cathedral is obtained with Gundulph's north tower in the foreground. On the opposite side of the road are a pair of weatherboarded seventeenth-century houses, restored by the council and now housing the Tourist Information Centre. Close to these lie Richard Watt's charity houses, founded in 1579 and restored in 1771 on the original lines. Here a night's lodging was offered for 'six poor travellers, not being rogues or proctors', a contraction of procurator, a religious vagrant of the day.

A little beyond here the High Street curves slightly and large sections of the restored town wall are visible, and further on lie two black and white half-timbered houses. Opposite these is Eastgate House, a superb early Tudor brick building, used by Dickens as a setting in many of his books and now used as a Dickens museum and centre.

Off the High Street, along Epaul Lane, lies Rochester's most important house historically, Restoration House. Dating largely from 1590 its main claim to fame is that King Charles II spent the night of 28th May 1660 here on his return from exile. Opposite the house are gardens known as the Vines, from the fact that the monks in the nearby abbey used this area as their vineyard. A footpath leads through them into the cathedral precincts passing en route Minor Canon Row, a splendid terrace of eighteenth-century houses, and the fourteenth-century Prior's Gate.

Following the cathedral close around, the route passes the remains of the abbey, destroyed during the Dissolution. Just above the castle moat opposite the cathedral lies Satis House, where Elizabeth I once stayed, and next door is Old Hall, a gabled and timbered house, in which Henry VIII is said to have waited impatiently for his first sight of Anne of Clèves on her arrival in England.

Amongst the historical buildings, Rochester has found room for a number of good pubs and restaurants as well as the other amenities that are expected in an urban area of this size.

12. Borstal to White Horse Stone

Buses: Borstal to Rochester; Bluebell Hill to Chatham and Maidstone.
Parking: car park at Bluebell Hill picnic area; also parking in Borstal and off Bluebell Hill.
Toilets: Bluebell Hill picnic area.
Pubs: White Horse at Borstal; Robin Hood at Common Road (garden, children's room).

Leaving the Medway Bridge turn right for about 20 yards, then left on a road alongside, but at a lower level than the M2. At a small Y junction bear right and continue between the buildings of Nashenden Farm with its twin oasthouses.

Oasthouses are still a familiar sight in Kent but are more likely to be desirable residences than used for their original purpose of drying hops. The circular oasthouse was first designed in 1835 and most of the existing ones date from this time. The roofs were covered with purpose-made tapered tiles to enable them to bed properly but later the circular form gave way to a square one enabling ordinary tiles to be used. These traditional methods for drying hops are rapidly being replaced by more efficient but less picturesque oil-fired drying sheds.

Leaving the farm road, the path continues along the edge of a field, shortly goes to the other side of the hedge and continues to the top of the field. To the right and looking back, there are fine views of the Medway valley and the noise of the motorway is reduced to a background hum insufficient to drown the singing of

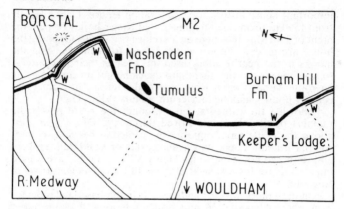

the skylarks.

Continuing on, a tumulus can be seen in the woodland to the left. The path passes through a small copse and comes to a junction with a footpath leading down to Wouldham, an unpicturesque village close to the Medway, with a mainly Gothic church. Walter Burke, the purser of HMS *Victory*, who held the dying Nelson in his arms, is buried in the churchyard and each year on Trafalgar Day a special service is held.

The path climbs again and the chalk ridge falls sharply away to the right; the view is mainly obscured by trees but a small clearing gives excellent views across the Weald. Continue on past the edge of Monk Wood (private) and in a short distance Keeper's Lodge is reached on the right. The path now changes to a loose stone road and continues to Burham Hill Farm. A public footpath sign points, rather prosaically, to Scarborough Terrace.

Continuing on, in ¼ mile the Robin Hood is reached on the left. To the right is a footpath to Burham, which straggles along the road lying below the Downs and was largely built to provide accommodation for the workers in the now disused quarries that scar the hillside. The original village lay closer to the river, near the Norman church, lying isolated amongst farmland with only farm buildings nearby. It is ironic that, having been deserted for the 'modern' church in Victorian times, the old church was brought back into service when the later one had to be pulled down in 1981 because the masonry was unsafe.

Continue along Common Road, passing two large houses, number 201 and Fairview, and shortly leave the road over a stile into Bluebell Hill picnic area and continue along the Downs past the car park and toilets provided for the picnic area. In a few hundred yards the path reaches the A229, almost opposite the

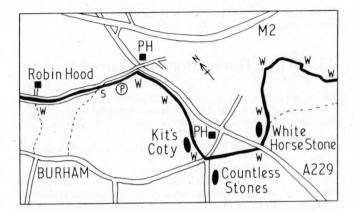

Upper Bell. The Way descends the hill alongside the road for about 300 yards and then diverges and runs at a lower level.

Continue down the hill and shortly turn down some steep concrete steps and along a tree-lined tunnel to the foot of the hill. Off to the right is Kit's Coty House in its commanding position overlooking the Medway.

Kit's Coty is the remains of a neolithic long barrow similar to the Coldrum Stones at Trottiscliffe. The earth mound has disappeared and what remains are three massive upright dolmens and a cross stone which once formed the entrance to the burial chamber. It has been suggested that the fascinating name is in some way connected with Catigern, the brother of the British chieftain Vortigern. The burial chamber was there at least two thousand years before Catigern existed but it is interesting that nearby Aylesford is the place at which in AD 455 Hengist and Horsa inflicted their defeat on the British under Vortigern.

Continue down the hill, crossing the Burham-Aylesford road, and along a path marked Pilgrims' Way. To the right, a few yards along the Aylesford road, lie the Countless Stones or Little Kit's Coty House. The fallen dolmens of another neolithic burial chamber, the name is derived from the manner in which they have fallen across one another, which makes it difficult to see where one stone ends and another begins.

Returning to the Pilgrims' Way, in ½ mile rejoin the road which crosses the A229 by a small underpass behind Cossington Service Station. Leave the road and rejoin Pilgrims' Way and, in about 150 yards, White Horse Stone can be seen in the woodland to the left. A large sarsen, it is believed to be the remains of another dolmen. In the upper right corner of the stone is a small hole and, with a liberal amount of imagination, it is said that the shape of a horse can be discerned with the hole as the eye.

13. White Horse Stone to Thurnham

Buses: Bluebell Hill to Chatham and Maidstone; Boxley to Maidstone; Detling to Maidstone and Faversham.
Parking: near Cossington Service Station; Boxley; Detling; a little at Thurnham.
Pubs: King's Arms at Boxley; Cock Horse at Detling (food).

From White Horse Stone continue along Pilgrims' Way for about 200 yards, then turn left into the wood. About 100 yards on the path arrives at a small clearing and here the waymarkers can be confusing. An arrow marking on a tree appears to indicate that the Way goes left along the foot of the hill but continue straight on and steeply up the hill through the woods. Shortly, the course is confirmed by waymarkers. In spring the woods are carpeted with bluebells, which give their name to nearby Bluebell Hill.

At the top of the hill the path enters a field, turns right and follows along the side of the wood. Although at a height of over 600 feet (183 metres), the view is mainly obscured by trees. Striding across the field are massive pylons and, where the cables descend the hill, a break has been made in the trees and there is a good view, although somewhat marred by the cables. Continue on, and in about 50 yards leave the field and continue along just inside the wood for about ½ mile.

The Way leaves the wood, re-enters the field and runs along to the left of a fenced pasture called Frog's Rough. At the edge of the pasture, turn right and continue along a road in front of Harp Farm. Where the road turns right down the hill towards Boxley, the Way continues straight on and enters Boxley Woods.

Boxley lies at the foot of the Downs, a delightful village consisting of a pub, a few scattered houses and a church which lies back from the road with a pretty green in front of it. The church is small and has an unusual entrance hall which was once the nave of the Norman church. When, in the thirteenth century, the original building became too small, a new church was built on to the east wall. Tennyson's sister, Cecilia, married Edmund Lushington in Boxley church and is buried in the Lady Chapel with other members of the Lushington family. Tennyson himself lived for some years at nearby Park House and the stream nearby is said to have inspired his poem 'The Brook'.

Opposite the church is the King's Arms and behind it lies a footpath leading to the remains of Boxley Abbey. Founded in

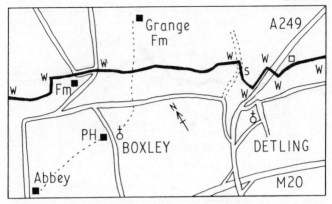

1146, this was the only Cistercian abbey in Kent and was famous in the middle ages for its miracle-working images. One was the Rood of Grace, an image of Christ on the Cross, which by movements of its body expressed pleasure or sadness depending on the size of a pilgrim's offering. It achieved notoriety at the dissolution when it was discovered that the movements were controlled by wires and it was publicly burned in St Paul's churchyard. Perhaps because of this, or because the adjudicators who decided against Henry's divorce from Catherine sat at Boxley, the abbey received particular attention at the dissolution. It was destroyed almost completely and all that remains are fragments of outer wall and a magnificent tithe barn dating from the thirteenth century.

Returning to the Way, continue through Boxley Woods along a path which, for 1¼ miles, is also a bridlepath and can be very muddy in wet weather. A break in the trees near Detling gives good views of the Weald and the face of an old chalk quarry which is known as Alpine Detling. Shortly after this, join, for a few yards, a track leading downhill and then go left across a stile into a field. Across the field, over another stile, turn left and descend steeply down the hillside to join the A249.

To the right, off the Way, lies Detling, which is entered past the Cock Horse, an attractive old pub. 'Cock horses' were kept at many pubs near hills to hitch to the front of coaches to assist with the ascent. Opposite the pub, on one corner of the road called Pilgrims' Way, is a Tudor wall and gateway, behind which once lay East Court, which has now been replaced by several modern houses. In the garden of one of these houses is a dovecot dating from Tudor times. Next to the gateway is a stone mounting block and on the other corner of the road is an old timber-framed building.

45

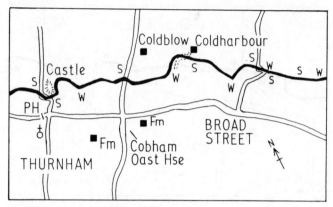

Returning to the Way, turn left uphill alongside the A249 and in ¼ mile, just before the crest of the hill, turn right across the main road. On the opposite side of the road, descend some concrete steps and turn left along the side of the hill. At a height of nearly 700 feet (650 metres) there are some superb views from here.

Follow the track uphill and then turn right behind the garden of a house and then along the side of a small copse. At the end of the copse go straight ahead across the field. Soon Thurnham church can be seen in the valley below.

The church is long, with a low turreted tower, and dates from Norman times with fourteenth-century additions. In the churchyard is the grave of Alfred Mynn, one of the fathers of Kent cricket, who died in 1861. There is also an interesting modern gravestone to a husband and wife who were local farmers. In black marble, it has on it two reproductions of old photographs of the couple in rural surroundings.

In a few hundred yards the path goes steeply downhill and straight ahead, following a line of trees, and then goes steeply uphill again. In ¼ mile cross a stile to join a road at Thurnham Castle.

Now covered with trees and brambles, this is the remains of a motte and bailey castle. Partly Norman, on the site of a much earlier castle, it was once held by Robert de Thurnham in the time of Henry II. From the top of the mound there are spectacular views of the Weald which demonstrate the effective defensive position the castle occupied.

Follow the road to the right around the base of the castle and rejoin the Way over a stile. To the right, further downhill along the road, lies Thurnham.

14. Thurnham to Harrietsham

Buses: Hollingbourne to Maidstone.
Trains: Hollingbourne to Maidstone and London (Victoria).
Parking: a little at Thurnham; car park at Hollingbourne station, and also near church.
Pubs: Black Horse at Thurnham; Pilgrim's Rest at Hollingbourne (food, garden).

From Thurnham, the Way can be joined by following the road uphill, passing on the left the Black Horse public house and on the right Thurnham Friars, a superb timber and brick building with herringbone pattern. Though looking perfectly Tudor, the house was built in the early part of the twentieth century but old timbers and bricks were used.

Continuing up the hill, the Way is rejoined at Thurnham castle. Turn right over a stile and follow the path to the left around the base of the castle. In ¼ mile turn right across the head of a small valley, then uphill and along the opposite side of the valley. Turn right along the edge of a wood and in a few yards turn left and follow the path steeply up into the wood. The Way continues through the wood and shortly goes steeply downhill and then up again by a series of wooden steps. At the top the path turns to the right along a broad track and then shortly joins a road.

Cross the road and continue straight ahead uphill and continue along the edge of a field for about ¼ mile. The path then runs steeply downhill to join a track running between two large fields. Turn left along the track and at the head of the field turn right and follow the path through the woods. In a few hundred yards, where the path divides, take the right fork over a stile and past a horse barrier; Coldharbour Farm lies to the left. The Way soon emerges from the wood and continues along the scarp of the hill with good views of Broad Street in the valley below.

Continue straight on through another wood and where the Way joins another path turn right along it for a few yards and then leave to the left. The Way continues straight ahead, crosses a field, goes over a stile into a small copse and then continues straight ahead along the edge of a field and in a few hundred yards crosses a stile to join a road which comes up from Broad Street, an attractive hamlet with some good buildings, including Brushings Farmhouse, a fine black and white Tudor house.

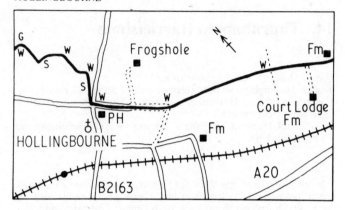

Returning to the Way, cross the road, go over a stile and continue straight ahead on a footpath through a wood. In about 300 yards leave the wood and continue along by the edge of the wood for about ¼ mile and then re-enter the wood. There seems to be no shortage of cowslips or rabbits in this area. Continuing on, the path reaches a wide bridlepath, which can be muddy. Turn left along it for about 100 yards and then leave to the right through a gate marked 'Private'. The Way continues on a wide track through the woods and then emerges again on to the open downs, and there are superb views from here over the Weald.

Continuing on, re-enter the woods for a short distance and then return to the open downs. The path descends the hill diagonally towards Hollingbourne which can be seen in the valley below. In about 200 yards, ignore the footpath straight ahead, turn left along the edge of the wood and then in a further 200 yards turn right down the hill. The path runs along the edge of a field for a short distance, then joins a narrow path between houses and shortly joins the road and runs down to Hollingbourne by the Pilgrim's Rest.

Hollingbourne is a pleasant village nestling below the downs and has some attractive buildings including several black and white half-timbered. The fifteenth-century church has numerous monuments to the Culpeper family, who lived at nearby Greenway Court. One of the treasures of the church is a beautiful embroidered altar cloth worked by the four daughters of the royalist Sir Thomas Culpeper in exile during the Commonwealth. Brought to the church at the Restoration, it is now only on display at church festivals.

The Way continues along a road to the left of the Pilgrims' Rest for about ¼ mile and then for a further ¼ mile along a track.

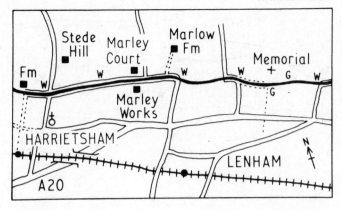

Leaving the track, continue on a path through woods and fields for about 1½ miles to join the road by Hillside Farm. To the right a wide track leads down to Harrietsham station. Continue along the road for 300 yards to the junction of the road leading down to Harrietsham. An attractive village, Harrietsham is cut in two by the A20 and unfortunately the best part lies south of the road. At the foot of the hill, however, lies the fourteenth-century church, which has an unusual Norman font. Above the porch is a sundial which is said to be accurate to five minutes.

15. Harrietsham to Charing

Buses: Harrietsham to Maidstone and Charing.
Trains: Harrietsham and Lenham to London (Victoria), Maidstone and Canterbury.
Parking: car park at Harrietsham station.
Pubs: Bank House and Roebuck Inn (food) at Harrietsham.

The Way crosses the road leading downhill to Harrietsham and continues along Pilgrims' Way. On the left are the landscaped gardens of Stede Hill and on the top of the hill is the lovely Georgian house restored by the author Robert H. Goodsall. Continuing on, the Way passes a few houses and the buildings of Whitegates Poultry Farm and shortly passes on the right the Marley Company factories and, on the left, Marley Court, from

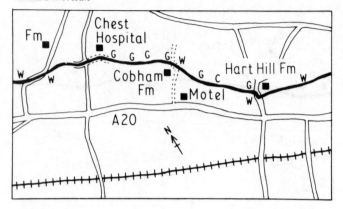

which the company took its name. It was formed during the First World War to make roof tiles to overcome a shortage of slates.

A short distance on, to the left, is Marlow Farm, named after the Canterbury family of which Christopher Marlowe, the playwright, was a famous member. Continue on, past a pleasant house called Dormans, and just beyond where the road turns right down to the A20 continue straight ahead along a footpath. In about ½ mile the path rejoins a road leading downhill to Lenham and in 200 yards leaves the road and continues along an access road in front of a few houses. At the last house, called House by the Cross, the Way passes through a gate into a field and runs along past the foot of Lenham's distinctive war memorial.

The turf has been cut from the hillside to expose the chalk in the shape of a huge cross, which is a clear landmark for travellers along the A20 below. At the foot of the cross a small iron cage once contained a memorial stone but this was removed to the church in 1960.

Continuing across the open downs, which are very exposed, the path enters a small spinney through a gate and continues on for ¼ mile and then joins a road. The Way continues along the road and where it bears left for Great Pivington Farm continue straight ahead along a footpath through a small wood. Shortly the path joins a small access road in front of some cottages, crosses the road leading up to Lenham Chest Hospital and runs along a footpath in front of the hospital grounds. Passing a small unobtrusive sewage works on the right, the path passes through a gate and then for about ¾ mile crosses through several fields with gates until it reaches Cobham Farm.

The Way bears right along the track for a few yards and then opposite the farmhouse turns left and runs by a narrow path with several gates along the edge of the fields for about 1 mile. Leaving the field through a gate, the path joins a road at Hart Hill Farm. Turn right for 100 yards, then leave the road to the left and continue through a small spinney.

The path rises gently towards Charing Hill about 1 mile ahead and shortly there are good views of Charing, with its superb Perpendicular church tower, lying at the foot of the downs. Leaving the spinney, the Way joins a wide track, passing on the left a new waterworks and on the right two houses, bears left past a house called Twyfords and a short distance on reaches the A252, which leads downhill to Charing.

Charing is fortunate in having been bypassed by the main Canterbury and Folkestone roads and this has enabled it to retain its pleasant appearance. The High Street is an attractive mixture of timber-framed, weatherboarded and Georgian brick buildings and the church, lying back from the road, has a fourteenth-century tower and a fine timbered roof with painted beams. Next to the church are the remains of the Tudor Archbishop's palace, where Cranmer once lived and where Henry VIII stayed on his way to the Field of the Cloth of Gold.

16. Charing to Boughton Lees

Buses: Charing to Maidstone, Canterbury and Folkestone.
Trains: Charing to London (Victoria), Maidstone, Folkestone and Canterbury.
Parking: car park at Charing station and near church.
Pubs: Queen's Head, Royal Oak, King's Head at Charing (food); Wheel Inn at Westwell (food, garden).

Crossing the A252, turn left and in 50 yards turn right along a road, marked Pilgrims' Way. The Way descends the hill slightly, past Lone Barn Farm, and in ½ mile passes, on the right, a road leading down to Pett Place. Continuing along the road, there are good views to the right and below can be seen the fine buildings of Pett Place, near which are the remains of a flint chapel. The Way continues on the road past Burnthouse Farm and just past the farmhouse bears left and then right along a road leading to a quarry. In the quarry on the left a bronze age burial site was found in 1935. Continue along a rough stone track and just past the quarry entrance, where the track divides, take the left fork. In 200 yards, where the path divides again, take the path straight ahead. The Way now runs straight ahead along a good path through a beechwood on the side of the ridge at about 500 feet (150 metres) and there are good views to the right.

Continue on the path for about 1 mile then join a wide rough

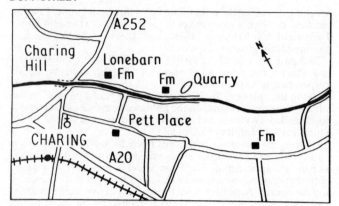

stone track and shortly a road and turn left along it. The Way continues along the road for ½ mile to the pretty hamlet of Dunn Street and in the valley below the village of Westwell can be seen.

Westwell is an attractive village set around a green and was mentioned in Domesday. It is said that the spring flowers bloom earlier here than for miles around. The church has a sixteenth-century porch and a carved wooden screen over five hundred years old. R. H. Barham, the author of the *Ingoldsby Legends*, was curate here from 1814 to 1817.

The Way continues past the few houses of Dunn Street, leaves the road over a stile and enters Eastwell Park, then runs along a wide track at the edge of a field with a small wood to the right. In ½ mile turn right through the narrow strip of wood and then turn left on the other side and continue along the edge of the wood. From here can be seen the lake covering over 40 acres (16 hectares) and the ruined church by the side of it. Continue along the edge of the wood and in 200 yards cross a stile and go straight across the field towards the church. Over to the left is Home Farm. On the other side of the field the Way crosses a stile on to a road and continues straight ahead. To the right is the lake and the church, which was hit by an incendiary bomb during the Second World War. Only the tower and ruined walls remain together with a few gravestones, one of which is reputed to be that of Richard Plantagenet, the bastard son of Richard III. He is said to have escaped after the battle of Bosworth and spent the rest of his life as a carpenter at Eastwell, his true identity only being revealed when he was an old man. By the side of the church on the edge of the attractive lake is Lake House, an unusually large thirteenth-century stone house with an upper hall. It is now being extensively restored.

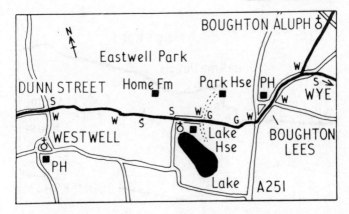

Continuing along the road through an avenue of poplar trees, in
¼ mile the Way leaves the road through a gate and continues
across a field. Over to the right behind some farm buildings is
Eastwell House; rebuilt several times, it is now in mock Tudor
style. Shortly, the path crosses diagonally to the left downhill and
runs along inside a fence beside the surfaced drive. In 100 yards,
go through a gate, cross over the drive, through another gate and
then continue diagonally right to emerge on to the A251 at the
apex of the triangular village green at Boughton Lees.

Crossing the A251, the Way runs along the road to the right of
the village green past some very attractive cottages. Ahead, to the
left, is the Flying Horse Inn, a good place to stop and watch the
cricket on summer weekends.

17. Boughton Lees to Chilham

Buses: Boughton Lees to Ashford; Chilham to Ashford and
    Canterbury.
Trains: Chilham to Ashford and Canterbury.
Parking: Boughton Lees and Chilham.
Pubs: Flying Horse at Boughton Lees (food, garden); White
    Horse at Chilham (food).

From the Flying Horse turn left and then left again along the
road for about ½ mile to the junction of the section of the Way
leading to Folkestone (see Section 22). Turn left along the section
to Canterbury and continue by a footpath for ½ mile to Boughton
Aluph church.

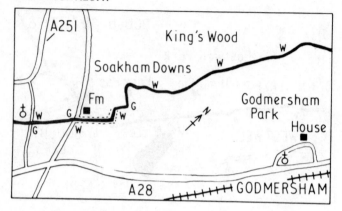

The large flint church lies isolated in the fields and has a thirteenth-century tower and a unique oak screen of the same date. It is said that the acoustics are very good and it has sometimes been used for recording purposes. In 1965 excavations near the church revealed a bronze-age burial site.

Past the church, the Way crosses a road and continues for nearly ½ mile across fields, then crosses another road and continues along a track past Soakham Farm.

Continue along the track, past the old farmhouse (now disused), for ½ mile, then leave to the right along a footpath. The path climbs steeply uphill giving good views and at the top of Soakham Downs enters Kings Wood, a part of Challock Forest.

The Way now runs for over 2 miles through Kings Wood and is pleasant walking. The path arrives at a Forestry Commission name board and just after this take the right-hand fork of the path and follow it downhill. Through the trees to the right there is a glimpse of the Palladian house of Godmersham Park. This is the property inherited by Jane Austen's brother, Edward, in 1797. Edward was adopted by the Knight family and changed his name in order to inherit the estate. Jane stayed many times at the house with her brother and a number of her letters were written from here.

The village church has a Norman tower and an unusual contemporary apse built out from it. Inside are some interesting monuments, including one to Edward Knight, and a twelfth-century bas-relief carving of a bishop, believed to be of Thomas à Becket. Near the gateway to Godmersham Park, the bridge over the river Stour was built in 1698.

Returning to the Way, the path continues downhill and ahead can be seen Hurst Farm with its twin oasthouses and nearby the timber-framed house. At the foot of the hill the path turns left and

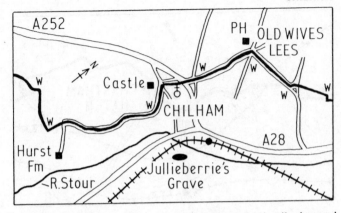

continues for 300 yards and then joins a road. In ½ mile the road passes through the attractive hamlet of Mountain Street. One of the houses is called Jullieberrie Cottage, a reminder of the neolithic long barrow, Jullieberrie's Grave, which is on the downs across the river valley.

The road continues for ¾ mile, passing on the left the walls of the grounds of Chilham Castle. Where the road bears right, continue straight ahead uphill into Chilham square.

Chilham is a lovely place which suffers for its attractiveness by the hordes of visitors in the summer. The castle sits at one end of the square and at the other end is the church. In between, the village square is lined with perfect timbered houses and from each corner of the square narrow roads lead off which are lined with attractive buildings.

The present castle was built in 1616 but retained parts of the original Norman keep. The house is not open to the public, but the grounds, designed by Capability Brown, are and in the summer displays of jousting and falconry complete the medieval atmosphere of the village.

The pleasant fifteenth-century church set in its lovely churchyard has some interesting monuments including one by the sculptor Sir Francis Chantrey (1781–1841). Sir Francis left his fortune to found the art collection which formed the basis of the Tate Gallery in London. One of the interesting items on display in the church is an old school table, carved and worn by generations of pupils and masters! Behind the church lies the attractive Georgian vicarage.

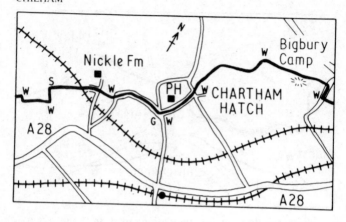

18. Chilham to Canterbury

Buses: Chilham to Canterbury and Ashford
Trains: Chilham and Chartham to Canterbury and Ashford.
Parking: Chilham, Old Wives Lees, Chartham Hatch.
Pubs: White Horse at Chilham (food); Star at Old Wives Lees;
   Chapter Arms at Chartham Hatch (food, garden).

From Chilham square the Way continues into the churchyard and bears left along a narrow path leading down to the road. Continue along the road, cross the A252 and follow the road ahead into Old Wives Lees, an attractively named village but undistinguished architecturally. At the road junction take the road diagonally right and continue through the village past many converted oasthouses and granaries. In ½ mile the Way bears left then shortly right and along a footpath through an orchard. The path continues through a hop field, then turns right and in 50 yards left by the edge of a field and climbs steeply uphill.

The path continues along the edge of the field for nearly ½ mile and then enters an orchard. From here there are good views across the Stour valley with orchards and hop fields stretching as far as the eye can see. The village of Chartham can be seen in the valley below. The Way continues through the orchard for ¼ mile then crosses the railway line and joins a farm road leading to Nickle Farm. Past the farm, continue straight ahead uphill along a narrow

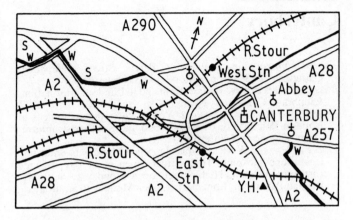

path and then join another farm road and continue along past the orchards for over ½ mile. Leave the farm road through a gate, turn left on the public road and in 20 yards turn right along New Town Street. Continue along the road into Chartham Hatch past the Chapter Arms. About 300 yards past the pub turn left at the road junction, then cross the road and take the narrow footpath to the right of a grocer's shop. The Way continues along the path, passing a children's playground, then continues through an orchard. Shortly, take the wide path to the left and in 200 yards turn right; in the valley the A2 can be seen and heard.

The Way continues along the path and in ¼ mile passes Bigbury Camp on the slopes above to the right. The covering of bracken and trees softens the outlines of the earth ramparts of this massive hillfort extending over 25 acres (10 hectares). The camp was used by the Belgic tribes in the area until the Romans established Canterbury as an administrative centre. There have been several archaeological finds, including Belgic pottery and metalwork, chariot equipment and iron slave chains.

Continue along the path and in ¼ mile cross over a stile on to a road. Turn left along the road and in a few yards follow the road across the bridge over the A2 Canterbury bypass. At the end of the bridge, turn right and follow the path beside the A2 and then in ¼ mile turn left down a narrow track. The path leads downhill and at the bottom continues straight ahead. Soon there are views of Canterbury ahead. Continue straight on to join the road and enter the outskirts of the city.

Canterbury

Tourist information centre: St Peters Street (telephone: Canterbury 66567), open Monday to Saturday only.

Buses: services to most parts of Kent and to London; information, telephone: Canterbury 63482.

Trains: two stations, East and West, with frequent services to London (Victoria or Charing Cross) and Kent coast; information, telephone: Canterbury 65151.

Places of interest: Westgate Museum, open Monday to Saturday; Eastbridge Hospital, High Street, open every day; Beaney Institute Museum, High Street, open Monday to Saturday; Roman Pavement, Longmarket, open Monday to Saturday.

Since the murder of Thomas à Becket in 1170, Canterbury has been a place of pilgrimage and still today to most visitors the cathedral is the main attraction. But the city was an administrative centre from Roman times and has secular buildings worthy of attention. To reach the cathedral one has to walk the narrow streets with their timbered and gabled houses and it is worthwhile stopping to look at some of these and appreciating the city as a whole.

The North Downs Way at present enters Canterbury just above Westgate. To the left along St Dunstans Street is the church of the same name, where Henry II changed into his penitent's clothes before walking barefoot to the cathedral. It is also the resting place of the head of Thomas More, brought here by his daughter after his execution in 1535 and buried in the family vault.

To the right, the city proper is entered through the superb Westgate. Set on the bank of the river, it is still serving its purpose as an entrance for traffic into the city. The upper floors are now used as a museum.

To the right of Westgate is the former church of the Holy Cross, given to the city by the Church Commissioners in 1972 and now used as a Guildhall.

Through the gateway the road becomes St Peters Street and a little way along on the left is the Tourist Information Centre. Further along on the same side lies the little church of St Peter the Apostle. The road continues to King's Bridge, over the river Stour, and to the left is the delightful Weavers House. Dating from 1500, this lovely gabled house was one of many taken over by Flemish Protestants fleeing persecution in their own country in the sixteenth century. Looking from the bridge along the side of the house, the town ducking stool can be seen. On the right of the river is the Eastbridge Hospital, founded as a hospice for poor pilgrims and still used as almshouses. Open to visitors, the hospital has a superb vaulted undercroft and a lovely restored fourteenth-century chapel.

Across the bridge the road becomes High Street and shortly on the left is the splendidly incongruous Victorian 'Tudor' building known as the Beaney Institute. Founded in 1891 with the money left by George Beaney, a Canterbury doctor who settled in Australia, it is now used as a museum and library.

Further along on the right is the little half-timbered house known as the Queen Elizabeth Guest Chamber. Now a pleasant restaurant and tea rooms, it has an excellent moulded ceiling dating from the sixteenth century. Almost opposite is Mercery Lane, running by the side of a well known chemist's shop, and down here is a good view of the cathedral. Before visiting the cathedral, however, turn right past some excavations of Roman foundations and the Marlowe Theatre and continue along to the castle.

The remains of the Norman keep are little more than a shell now but it must have been at one time as impressive as that at Rochester. On the left is a narrow footpath leading to the restored city walls which follow the line of the original Roman city. A short distance along is the Dane John mound and the municipal gardens below it. The name is a corruption of 'donjon' (a Norman keep) but it is doubtful if this was its original purpose. On top of the mound is a pillar with an inscription which explains how the city fathers of the nineteenth century gave this open space to the people in perpetuity.

In the gardens is a monument to Christopher Marlowe, the poet and playwright, who was born and educated in Canterbury. Marlowe was only twenty-nine when he was murdered in a pub brawl in Deptford.

Further along the wall at St George's Gate leave the wall and enter 'modern' Canterbury, the new shopping area built to replace the area lost during the bombing in the Second World War. Near the wall is the tower of St George's, all that remained after the blitz of the church in which Marlowe was baptised in 1564. A little further on is the shopping precinct Longmarket and under the restaurant are a Roman mosaic and remains of a hypocaust on view to the public.

Continue to the right along Butchery lane, and then left into Burgate. Shortly, the timbered buildings of the Buttermarket can be seen and nearby Christ Church Gate leading to the Cathedral precinct.

Canterbury has been the centre of Christianity in England since Saxon times but without the vast sums of money that poured in from pilgrims after Becket's murder it would probably never have become so magnificent. The soaring Bell Harry Tower, which is familiar to most from thousands of pictures, was added in the late fifteenth century and represents almost the last addition from pilgrims' funds before the Dissolution. The main attraction for pilgrims, Becket's shrine, is no longer here, having been destroyed and its treasures removed by Henry VIII's commissioners.

Outside and inside, the cathedral is a collection of many architectural styles merging into one magnificent building. The crypt, however, is still largely the original Norman begun by Archbishop Lanfranc and completed by Anselm. Many thousands of words have been written about the cathedral but the best way to appreciate it is as was originally intended, just go and look.

19. Canterbury to Bishopsbourne

Buses: Bekesbourne, Patrixbourne and Bridge to Canterbury.
Trains: Bekesbourne to Canterbury East and London (Victoria) or Dover.
Parking: Longport (Canterbury).
Pubs: in Canterbury only.
Toilets: Longport (Canterbury).

The North Downs Way starts again at St Martin's Hill. To get there from the city walls, walk down St George's Place (A2) from the roundabout close to the bus station. Turn left along Lower Chantry Lane (A257) to the junction with Longport, by some public lavatories. Straight ahead are the remains of St Augustine's Abbey and St Augustine's College. The abbey was started in 598 by St Augustine and he and the early archbishops were buried there. The Saxon buildings were levelled in 1070 to allow the building of a great church, which was in turn demolished at the Dissolution. Part of it was incorporated into a palace for Henry VIII. St Augustine's College, a Victorian missionary college, incorporates the abbey gatehouse, the Fyndon Gate, where Charles I and Queen Henrietta Maria spent their wedding night.

Turn right along Longport to pass the Sessions House and jail, both built in 1808. On the right is the eighteenth-century Barton Court, now a school, and a group of almshouses endowed in 1644 by a couple after the birth of a son after twenty years of childless marriage.

On the left, a few yards down North Holmes Road, is the oldest

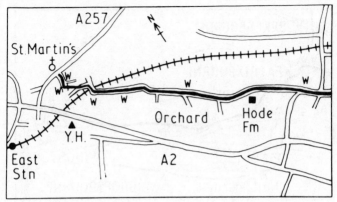

surviving church in England, St Martin's. It was described by the Venerable Bede as the place where Queen Bertha, the wife of Ethelbert, worshipped in the sixth century before the coming of St Augustine to Kent. Augustine, before he converted King Ethelbert, had his headquarters at St Martin's. The building contains many Roman bricks and parts of it may have been built during the Roman occupation, although most of it is of the seventh century.

Just past the church the Way goes down Spring Lane and after 50 yards turns right into Pilgrims' Way, then keeps left in front of some tennis courts with St Martin's windmill, built in 1816, up to the left. A road joins from the right and then the Way crosses a railway bridge and goes through a housing estate. At the far end the Way runs into a private road, through an orchard, for about a mile, keeping left at a fork and being joined by a road from the right, and then passes Hode Farm, with a brick gabled end and parts dating from 1674. The oasthouse and barn are being sold for conversion into dwellings. The Way continues through the orchard and then runs downhill, through some trees to a road.

Turn left into the road and then right at the roundabout down into Patrixbourne. ½ mile to the north is Bekesbourne, a small village where a Tudor palace once stood. The gatehouse that remains was where Cranmer wrote part of the Common Prayer Book. Just outside the village is John Aspinall's zoo, Howletts.

Patrixbourne may be the site of the battle in which Julius Caesar defeated the Britons on his second invasion of the country. The charming village has some neo-Georgian houses but the Tudor style, largely nineteenth-century, predominates. The church, at the far end of the village, has a magnificent Norman doorway, possibly carved by the masons that worked on Rochester

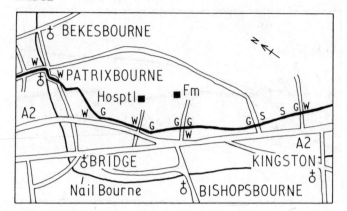

Cathedral, and some fine Swiss stained glass.

Just past the church the Way turns left into a field and bears right to run parallel with the road for 100 yards and then turns left along the edge of the field. Ahead, behind the A2, is the village of Bridge, which consists mainly of modern housing. The church was largely rebuilt in 1859 but incorporated a Norman doorway.

At a gate the Way turns left to run along a path beside the A2 with an orchard to the left. Over to the left is Highland Court, a stone house built in 1904 for Count Zabrowski, the racing motorist of 'Chitty-Chitty-Bang-Bang' fame. It is now a hospital.

By the Elham turn-off sign on the A2 turn left through a gate, cross a field diagonally and then go along its edge up to the road that, to the right, runs under the A2 into Bishopsbourne.

The rector of Bishopsbourne from 1595 to 1600 was Richard Hooker, whose book *The Laws of Ecclesiastical Pollity* was partly instrumental in moderating the views of the Elizabethan church. The Georgian rectory, now called Oswalds, was the home of Joseph Conrad for the final years of his life. The church has a stained glass window by William Morris and Burne-Jones and some medieval wall paintings.

20. Bishopsbourne to Shepherdswell

Buses: Barham to Canterbury and Dover.
Trains: Snowdown to Canterbury East and London (Victoria) or Dover.
Parking: on roads only.

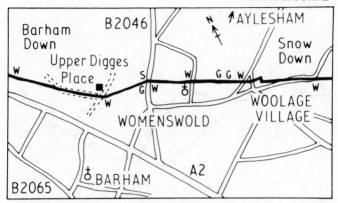

The Way crosses the road from Bishopsbourne just north of the A2 into a field opposite. To the right, on the far side of the A2 is Charlton Park. The partly Tudor house was altered in 1790 for John Foote, a close friend of the Prince Regent. The ballroom was especially built so the Prince could relax with amateur dramatics after reviewing troops on Barham Downs. The Prince also used the house when courting Lady Conyingham, one of the family that occupied Bifrons in Patrixbourne until the mid twentieth century.

The Way runs through the field and in about 1 mile crosses a minor road into another field. At the far side of this field a concrete road is crossed into another field. On the other side of the A2 is Kingston, a quiet village with both old and new houses. The church contains a thirteenth-century font that was rescued in 1775 from use as a pig trough.

A track joins the Way from the left. Over to the left is Aylesham, a dreary mining village built in the 1920s for the miners of the Snowdown Colliery. The Way reaches Upper Digges Place on Barham Downs. The Downs have through history been used for the assembly of armies. In the Napoleonic Wars a huge camp for troops was established here to match a similar army behind Boulogne. A windmill that stood close to the house was burnt down in 1970.

The way crosses a track and passes a house. Before it reaches the next road the Way forks left off the track to a stile on to a road. Across the road the path runs up the side of a field for about ⅓ mile to some farm buildings. On the other side of the farmyard the Way comes out on a road by Womenswold church. The attractive thirteenth-century church contains a number of memorials, one of which incorporates a very realistic carving of a skull looking out over the pews. Close to the church there are

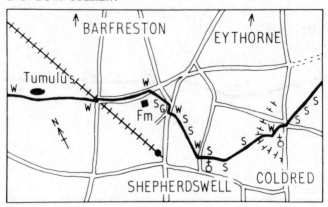

several eighteenth-century cottages.

The Way crosses into a track beside a house opposite the church and then in 20 yards keeps left of a fence up the side of a field and goes through two gates. Over to the left is the winding gear of the Snowdown Colliery, the most successful of the four collieries in East Kent and where serious mining began in 1913. At the end of the fields the Way crosses a road and goes through some trees for a few yards to a second road. Turn right and then left down the edge of a field before the crossroads at Woolage Village, which is just a collection of rather drab housing. If this field is ploughed it may be easier to turn left at the crossroads and walk along the road. The Way joins this road just before a sharp left-hand bend.

The Way keeps straight on at the bend of the road, up a path. At the top the path passes close to a tumulus and then descends ½ mile to a road by a railway bridge. On the other side of the bridge the Way turns right down a road signposted to Eythorne. Barfreston, a mile to the north, has a Norman church famous for its marvellous carvings. The Way in about ½ mile turns right, off the road, down a path beside Longlane Cottage. In ¼ mile this path reaches a road where the Way turns right to cross a level crossing. Just past the crossing the Way goes up a narrow path, crosses a little road and goes over some fields towards an estate of modern bungalows. Beside the bungalows it goes down a track into Mill Lane with Shepherdswell village green a few yards down to the right.

The name Shepherdswell is a folk corruption of Sibert's Wold, which it is still sometimes called. It is possible it is connected with the Saxon king Sibert, who founded Westminster Abbey. The church was built in the 1860s on the foundations of an older one that was demolished.

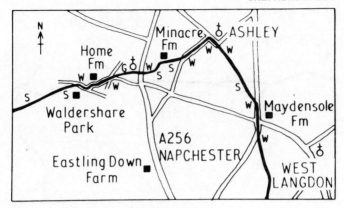

21. Shepherdswell to Dover

Buses: Shepherdswell to Dover; Waldershare Park to Dover.
Trains: Shepherdswell to Canterbury East and London (Victoria) or Dover.
Parking: on roads only.
Pubs: White Hall (garden), Bricklayers' Arms, Bell Inn at Shepherdswell; Butchers' Arms at Ashley.

The North Downs Way leaves Shepherdswell down a path opposite the school in Mill Lane, crosses two stiles and then goes over another to continue on the left of a fence. It crosses a stile by a gate and cuts diagonally left across a field to another stile and similarly over the next field. In the far corner of this field there is a cutting in an embankment that carried a section of the East Kent Railway to a now disused mine. On the far side the Way passes along the edge of a field and then bears left behind the seventeenth-century Coldred Court and Coldred church. The little church of St Pancras is built on an earthworks, probably the site of a Roman camp. The broken bell hanging on the gable is reputed to be one of the oldest in Britain.

The Way turns right along the road past the church to a crossroads, where it crosses to a path to the left of the road running straight ahead. The path leads through some trees and across the fields of Waldershare Park. Over to the right is a massive brick summerhouse built by Sir Robert Furnese in 1725.

The park was part of the property that Bishop Odo, the brother of William the Conqueror, held in Kent. It is now the seat of the Earl of Guildford. The path runs straight across the fields, taking

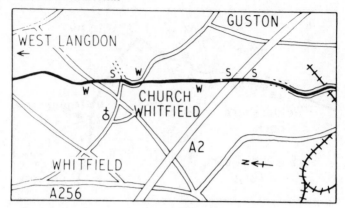

some steps over a fence, and then across a field to a stile in front of the Queen Anne mansion. It was built for Sir Henry Furnese, who died in 1712 just before it was completed. The house was gutted and refitted in 1913 and has recently been converted to accommodate luxury flats.

The Way goes down to the left of the house and just past the garages turns left and then right, by a cottage, along the driveway. In about 200 yards, at a crossroads, the Way goes into the field opposite and crosses it, diagonally to the left, to a stile by a white gate. On the other side is the churchyard of All Saints' church, with its bell hanging on a gable outside. The church contains some interesting monuments but it is generally locked.

The Way runs beside the church and straight across the road into a field. Over a stile it turns left and then by Minacre Farm turns right by going over two other stiles into a small field and then over a stile into a track coming up from the farm. It continues between some gateposts and up a field to a minor road, turns left along the road and after ¼ mile turns right through the village of Ashley. Where the road bears left the Way keeps straight on down a track. The track leads over a hill and in ½ mile reaches another minor road, running along the line of the old Roman road from Canterbury to Dover. The Way turns right along the road and goes straight across a crossroads and then after 50 yards turns left along a path. The path runs through Cane Wood, and after ¾ mile reaches a road running to Whitfield. As the road is approached a partly Saxon church (almost completely rebuilt in 1894), a little way out of Whitfield, can be seen over to the right. At the road the Way turns right along the old road, now a lay-by, and straight across the new road into a path. In ¼ mile it comes out at another road where the Way turns left. In a few yards the road bends right

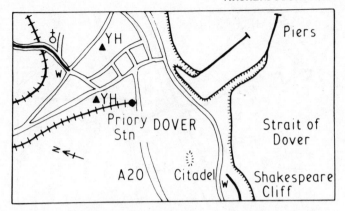

at a junction with a private road, then to the left. In about 100 yards, where the road bears left, the Way goes off to the right down a track along the line of the Roman road. The slope rising up to the right is Archers Court Hill. It is said that the knight who held the manor of Archers Court was required to accompany the King when he travelled abroad and to hold a silver bowl should the monarch be a poor sailor.

The Way crosses the new A2. Over to the left as the path climbs uphill the clock tower of the Duke of York's Royal Military School in Guston, dating from 1909, can be seen. The name Guston is probably derived from 'Goose Town' because a goose fair was held here in the middle ages. The path leads into a track and then into a road, which drops downhill to Charlton Cemetery, on the outskirts of Dover, and the end of the Way. The road can be followed straight on down into Frith Road, and central Dover.

22. Boughton Lees to Brabourne

Buses: Boughton Lees and Wye to Ashford and Canterbury.
Trains: Wye to Canterbury and Ashford.
Parking: Boughton Lees and Wye.
Pubs: Flying Horse at Boughton Lees; Tickled Trout (food), George Inn and King's Head at Wye.

From the Flying Horse, turn left and in 100 yards turn left again along the road. Continue along, passing the junction of the section of the Way leading to Canterbury (see sections 17–18). Where the road bears sharp left, leave to the right over a stile and continue

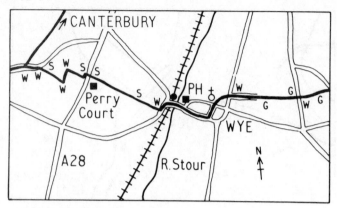

along the edge of fields for about ½ mile until the path reaches the A28. There are good views of the downs and a huge crown cut into the chalk above Wye.

Leaving the field, cross the road and continue straight ahead through an orchard past Perry Court Farm. Continue across fields, with several stiles, for about ¾ mile and then join a road. Turn left, and in 200 yards turn right over the level crossing by Wye station and continue along, crossing the bridge over the river Stour. To the right of the bridge is an attractive white boarded mill house with a weir next to it and to the left the Tickled Trout.

Continue along Bridge Street and then turn left into Church Street, a wide straight street with numerous attractive buildings, which runs to the church. Wye is a dignified little town and was the scene of the official opening ceremony of the North Downs Way by the Archbishop of Canterbury in September 1978. It was also the birthplace of Aphra Amis-Behn, who was baptised in the church in 1640. A colourful character, she was the first Englishwoman to become a professional writer and is said to have acted as a spy for Charles II.

The church is a strange collection of styles with a short, broad tower which replaced an earlier spire struck by lightning. It was a collegiate foundation endowed by Cardinal Kempe in 1444 and the college now forms part of the Agricultural School of London University.

The Way runs diagonally right, through the churchyard and behind the college buildings, then crosses a road and continues straight ahead for ½ mile past the greenhouses and experimental plots of the college. At the edge of the grounds, cross a road, continue across a field then over a stile, and follow a narrow path which runs steeply up through the woods. At the top turn right

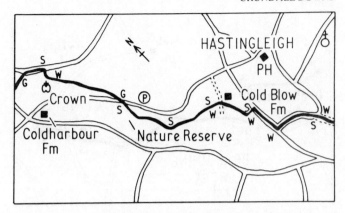

along a road and then shortly leave to the right over a stile and follow the path to emerge on the top of the downs overlooking Wye. Below is the enormous crown, cut by students from Wye College to commemorate the coronation of Edward VII in 1902.

The Way continues to the left over the top of the downs and there are superb views. In about ¾ mile cross a road, then go over a stile to enter the Wye and Crundale Downs National Nature Reserve, 'established to maintain a good example of chalk downland and woodland and its characteristic flora and fauna'. The path continues through a small wood on to the open downs, which fall away spectacularly at this point. Continuing across the downs, keeping to the edge of the ridge, the path leaves the nature reserve and continues along the edge of fields to Cold Blow Farm. Fanciful interpretations have been given for the names Cold Blow and Cold Harbour, which occur in many places on the Pilgrims' Way. On a winter's day, however, the former name is self-explanatory and Cold Harbour is believed to be a place, sometimes the ruins of a Roman villa, in which pilgrims could shelter from the wind.

Continue across the fields past Cold Blow and in ¼ mile cross a stile and go diagonally left across the field to join a road. To the left the road leads to Hastingleigh, a small village beautifully situated on the downs, with a thirteenth-century flint church, set some distance from the village. Turn right along the road and in ¼ mile turn left and continue along the road. In about 600 yards, where it turns sharp left, continue straight ahead along a track through lovely downland countryside for about ¾ mile and then join another road. Turn right, and in ¼ mile, where the road turns sharp left, in the field ahead is a triangulation pillar. Follow the road round and downhill slightly, and then where it turns right leave through a gate on to a track. Continue along the track for

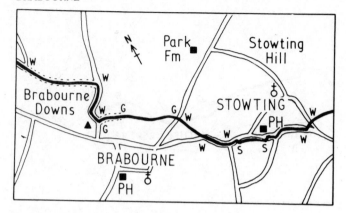

300 yards, then go through a gate and join a narrow path running through the edge of a wood above a disused quarry. The path continues for ½ mile climbing gently and then reaches a road which leads downhill to the right to Brabourne.

A small, attractive village set at the foot of the downs, Brabourne has an interesting church with some Norman features. In the squat, massive tower is a rough-hewn oak ladder, the sides of which are made from a single tree and are over 31 feet (9.5 metres) long. In the north wall by the altar is a window with original twelfth-century glass, believed to be the oldest complete window left in England. Nearby there is a 'heart-shrine' believed to be of John de Baliol, founder of Balliol College, Oxford, who died in 1269.

23. Brabourne to Etchinghill

Buses: Brabourne Lees (1½ miles south of Brabourne) to Maidstone, Charing and Folkestone.
Parking: Brabourne; Stowting; car park at Monks Horton picnic area; Postling.
Pubs: Five Bells at Brabourne; Anchor Inn at Stowting (food, garden).

The Way crosses the road and continues downhill on a track for ¼ mile to join another road. Turn left along the road and continue along to the outskirts of Stowting. A road off the Way to the left leads to the centre of this attractive village, which has a much restored fourteenth-century church with a contemporary timbered

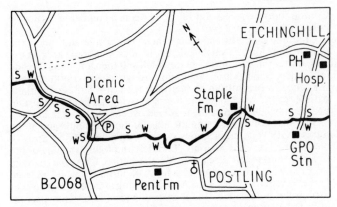

porch. On the hill above the village Saxon burial mounds have been found.

The Way continues straight ahead and shortly leaves the road to the right and runs along the edge of the field parallel to the road for 300 yards. If the field is ploughed, it can be uncomfortable walking, and it is easier to continue straight along the road. The path leaves the field opposite the Anchor Inn, turns right and continues along the road past the attractive buildings of Water Farm. ¼ mile past the farm, turn left off the road on a path running steeply uphill and in 50 yards cross another road. Continue straight on, steeply uphill to the top of Cobbs Hill, and from the top are very good views. The Way runs straight ahead over some stiles and in ¼ mile reaches the B2068, turns right and continues along the edge of fields, over several stiles, parallel to the road. This is Stane Street, the Roman road which runs in an almost straight line from Canterbury to the Roman port of Lympne (pronounced Limm).

Continue along the edge of the field and in ½ mile pass the picnic area at Monks Horton. About 300 yards further on cross the road and continue straight ahead across a field. Soon the sea can be seen for the first time and on the horizon the buildings of Dungeness power station, one of the first nuclear power stations built. The Way continues across the field for ¼ mile, then crosses a stile, runs downhill straight ahead and in 300 yards bears left uphill. Turn right at the telegraph pole and follow the path by the side of the fence; shortly, there are good views of the small village of Postling and the attractive twelfth- and thirteenth-century church with its shingled spire. There is an unusual dedication stone in the church giving the exact day but, intriguingly, no year. Just to the right of the village is Pent Farm, which was rented by Joseph

Conrad, between 1898 and 1907. He wrote a number of his novels here, including *Lord Jim*.

Continue along by the fence, then cross a stile and follow the path by the side of a small spinney. In a few hundred yards, at the end of the spinney, turn right downhill and then left along the side of a fence. In 300 yards turn right through a gate, continue along the fence to the bottom of the field, then turn left and continue parallel to the road to Staple Farm. Leaving the field over a stile, bear right slightly, cross the road and over a stile into a field.

The Way continues along the edge of the field uphill and at the top is a GPO communications station with an impressive array of dish-shaped receiving aerials. Turn left and follow the line of the fence around to the access road for the station. Cross the road, go over a stile and continue along a footpath through a wood. A large notice reveals that this is an 'MOD training area, including use of explosives, blanks, etc', but it gives no indications of any precautions to be taken.

The path continues along the edge of the wood for 500 yards and there is then a good view to the right of the symmetrical cone-shaped contours of Summerhouse Hill. Shortly, the path turns left over a stile and continues for nearly ½ mile through the edge of the wood to B2065, which leads to the left into Etchinghill.

An unprepossessing village, Etchinghill is distinguished by the large hospital which dominates most of the village.

24. Etchinghill to Folkestone

Buses: Etchinghill to Folkestone and Canterbury.
Trains: Folkestone to Dover and London (Charing Cross).
Parking: Etchinghill and Folkestone.
Pubs: New Inn at Etchinghill; Cat and Custard Pot at
    Paddlesworth; Valiant Sailor at Dover Hill (food, garden).

Cross the B2065, turn right and in a few yards left along a narrow road leading to Coombe Farm. In 100 yards leave the road to the left over a stile and continue diagonally right downhill across a field. Ahead can be seen the brick arches and embankment of a disused railway; this was the direct Canterbury to Folkestone line.

The Way continues down the field and in the right-hand corner crosses a stile and enters a wood. In a short distance turn left through the brick archway of the railway and continue straight ahead across a field. The path crosses a stile into a spinney and in 200 yards continues straight ahead over rough pasture and climbs steeply uphill. At the top of the hill turn right and continue along the edge of the fence. Shortly, the path crosses a stile and there are

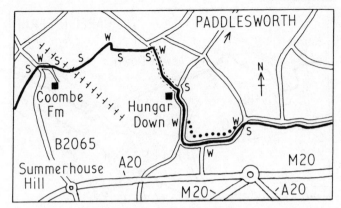

good views of the sea and coastline with the broad sweep of St Mary's Bay in the distance. Turn left, continue along the line of the fence and then along the edge of a field for ¼ mile.

Cross over a stile and turn right along a narrow track between hedges for ½ mile to join a road which, to the left, leads to Paddlesworth. A small village at the top of the downs, Paddlesworth has a tiny Norman flint church. The nave is less than 50 feet (15 metres) long by 20 feet (6 metres) wide and the chancel proportionately minute. The nearby pub is unusually named the Cat and Custard Pot.

The Way turns right down the road, passing the driveway of Hungar Down, and shortly reaches another section where rights have not been negotiated. Continue along the road, ignoring two roads off to the right, for nearly a mile to rejoin the designated Way just before a Y junction. A few yards before the junction, leave the road to the right over a stile and continue along the top of the downs parallel to the road. The path continues along the downs for ¾ mile with good views of Folkestone ahead and then runs along a narrow path between fences. Continue along the path for ¼ mile, past the Dover and Folkestone Quarantine Kennels, to the road. Cross the road, go over a stile and follow the path to the right around Castle Hill, an enormous motte and bailey castle. Known locally as Caesar's Camp, the exact date is unknown but it is more likely to be medieval than Roman.

From the castle are superb views along the coast and on a clear day the coastline of France can be seen. In the foreground is the smooth, grassy, cone-shaped Sugar Loaf Hill, which is apparently man-made, but when or why is unknown. The Way continues around Castle Hill, crosses over the top of Round Hill and runs straight ahead to join a road a few yards from the A260. Continue

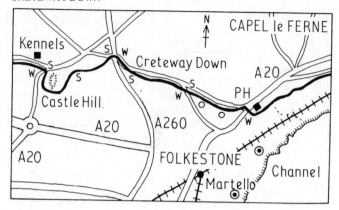

along the road, cross the A260 and go straight ahead along Crete Road East. In about 300 yards leave the road to the right over a stile and continue along the top of Creteway Down parallel with the road. Soon there are good views of Folkestone harbour and on the cliffs nearby two martello towers. A chain of these towers, each surmounted with a gun, was erected in 1804 along the south coast as part of the coastal defences. Later, in the 1820s, they were used to accommodate members of the Coast Blockade, a naval force set up to combat smuggling and the forerunner of the present Coast Guard.

Running through the centre of the town is the splendid railway viaduct built by William Cubitt in 1843. The nineteen slender brick piers carry the railway 100 feet (30 metres) above the Foord valley. According to Defoe Folkestone was a 'miserable fishing village' and apparently it remained so until the coming of the railways turned it into a fashionable seaside resort. There is little of great architectural interest in the town but some parts of the fishing village remain in the harbour area and there are some pleasant houses along the Lees which run for over a mile along the clifftops.

William Harvey, the discoverer of blood circulation, was born in Folkestone in 1578 and there is a memorial window to him in the parish church of St Mary. Several authors and artists have lived in the town, including Dickens and H. G. Wells, who wrote several of his novels here including *Kipps* and *The History of Mr Polly*.

Returning to the Way, the path continues along the top of Creteway Down passing two pillboxes left from the Second World War, which contrast with their earlier counterparts on the cliff below. Continue along the path to join the A20 at the top of Dover Hill. Opposite is the Valiant Sailor public house.

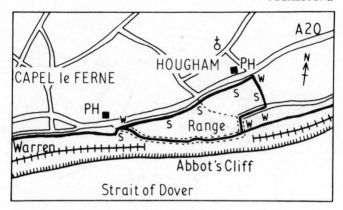

25. Folkestone to Dover

Buses: along A20 to Dover or Folkestone.
Parking: car park at Royal Oak.
Pubs: Valiant Sailor, Royal Oak, Plough Inn (garden).
Toilets: near Royal Oak.

The North Downs Way goes down a footpath a few yards on the Folkestone side of the Valiant Sailor. The path leads to the cliff-top, with a splendid view down over Folkestone and a martello tower. Close to the tower is the site of a Roman villa. Excavations in 1924 unearthed a number of pottery remains and Roman coins that had been minted in London.

The path turns left along the clifftop. It passes another path that winds down to the cliff base known as The Warren. The gault clay, which underlies the chalk, is impervious to the water that seeps down through the cliffs. This has made it act as a slide, so the cliffs have slipped into a broken landscape here. Further east, at Dover, the gault clay is below sea level and the cliffs drop straight into the sea. The Warren is rich in the fossils associated with gault clay.

The Way runs along the clifftop, going down and up a steep gulley and behind a house called Eagle's Nest. It then continues on the seaward side of some modern bungalows until, about ¾ mile from the Valiant Sailor, it joins the clifftop road in the residential village of Capel-le-Ferne. The road passes a tiny café and then past the Capel Court Country Club the Way keeps right. After passing another café it continues through a camp site and then behind Abbotscliffe House.

75

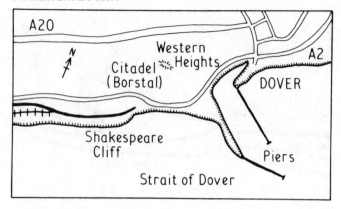

The route the Way takes here depends on whether the Army are using the Lydden Spout rifle range. If they are not firing, the Way continues along a track on the clifftop with the French coast visible over the Channel on a clear day. However, if a red flag is flying a path through the fields beside the A20 must be taken. Unfortunately it is little used so it is often overgrown. In 1¼ miles, with the ITA transmitter at Hougham over to the left, it reaches the Plough Inn, where it turns right uphill. It crosses a stile at the top, then runs down the edge of a field to a minor road. It turns right along the road for ¼ mile, then goes left to pass some gutted brick buildings. At the clifftop it reaches the track that has come along past the rifle range.

The path continues along the clifftop the 2 miles to Aycliff. The cliff here is known as Shakespeare's Cliff because it has been associated with the cliff near Dover which the blind Gloucester tried to jump over in *King Lear*. Edgar, describing the cliff, mentions a samphire gatherer halfway down the face. The fleshy leaves of samphire were collected until the nineteenth century for use in a pickle. The gatherers were sometimes lowered down the cliff face by ropes. Today bits of the cliff are sometimes sent overseas as souvenirs. The railway line, which runs along the base of the cliff at The Warren, has to run here through a tunnel and the path passes several air shafts.

Over to the left, on the other side of the housing estate, on the Western Heights is one of the strongest fortifications ever built. It was begun in the Napoleonic Wars and was resumed in the 1850s. In event of invasion it was supposed to have housed a beleaguered army, behind the enemy, that could be used to cut their lines of communication. Cobbett regarded it as a squandering of money and materials and argued that its purpose would be useless when the enemy had many other suitable landing places. The fort's citadel is now used as a borstal.

Above Aycliff the path descends down to the road, past some allotments, and to the end of the North Downs Way. The road runs past the docks and joins the A20 on the seafront at Dover.

Dover

Tourist information: Townwall Street (telephone: Dover 205 108), open every day; Town Hall, High Street (telephone: Dover 206941); open Monday to Friday only, but Saturdays also June to September.

Buses: Bus Station, Penchester Road (telephone: Dover 206813), services to most parts of Kent.

Trains: Priory Station (telephone: Dover 201753), services to London (Victoria and Charing Cross) and most parts of Kent.

Places of interest: Castle, open every day except Good Friday and Christmas Day; Maison Dieu and Museum, High Street, open weekdays only; Roman Painted House, New Street, open every day except Mondays, March to November; St Edmund's Chapel, Priory Road, open every day.

For two thousand years Dover has been known as the 'Key to England' and it is easy to see why. Situated at the shortest distance between the French and English coasts, with distinctive white cliffs either side of a river that was navigable well inland until Norman times, it was inevitable that Dover should be a tempting landing place. Julius Caesar received such a hot reception from the locals when he tried to land that he made for Deal further up the coast. However, in the first century AD the invading Romans set up a fort and two lighthouses on the clifftops either side of the river Dour. A succession of forts was built on the cliffs from pre-Roman times, but the existing castle is largely that built for Henry II in the 1180s. Set impressively on the eastern cliffs, it dominates the approaches to the harbour.

Inside the castle are the remains of the Pharos, one of the Roman lighthouse towers. Originally over 100 feet (30 metres) high, only about 40 feet (12 metres) remain but this makes it the tallest Roman building in Britain. Also inside the castle is the church of St Mary-in-Castro. Originally a Saxon foundation, it was extensively restored in the nineteenth century. The underground workings in the castle, dating from Norman to Napoleonic times, are well worth seeing.

Behind the castle, on the clifftop, there is a memorial to Bleriot, who on 25th July 1909 made history with the first cross-channel flight. Below the castle, on Marine Parade, is a statue to Charles Stewart Rolls, who less than a year later capped Bleriot's achievement by flying to France and back. Nearby is a memorial to another solo crossing, a bust of Captain Matthew Webb, who in August 1875 after twenty-two hours in the water became the first person to swim the Channel.

A walk along Marine Parade is a good way to get an impression of the size of Dover harbour with its constant succession of boats and hovercraft which carry thousands of passengers into and out of Britain each year. However, although Dover had been the premier port on the south coast for centuries, it was only at the beginning of the twentieth century that the decision was made to make it large enough to shelter the entire home fleet.

Behind the harbour, little remains architecturally of Dover's history, the cross-channel shelling during the Second World War and subsequent redevelopment having taken their toll. Along Cannon Street is the parish church of St Mary. Largely rebuilt in the nineteenth century, it retains its Norman tower. Just off Cannon Street, in New Street, is the Roman Painted House. Discovered in 1970, it has been saved from the fate of having a multi-storey car park built on it and is now on display in a covered exhibition room. These are the most extensive remains of a Roman painted house yet found in Britain and are thought to be the best example north of the Alps. Many Roman and medieval sites were excavated during the recent redevelopment but most of them have been buried again and are now covered with new roads and buildings.

Further along High Street is the incongruous Victorian town hall which incorporates parts of the thirteenth-century Maison Dieu. This once extensive building was a hospital for pilgrims and travellers but was closed at the Dissolution. It now houses the town museum, which has displays of general interest and local history. Next to the town hall is Maison Dieu House, a Dutch gabled house built in 1665 and now housing the public library. Behind this are Maison Dieu Gardens, from which there is a good view of the castle on the hill above.

Near the town hall, in Priory Road, is St Edmund's Chapel. This small, attractive chapel was consecrated in 1253 and dedicated by St Richard of Chichester to his friend St Edmund, who was the first divinity student at Oxford. It is the only English chapel dedicated by one saint to another. The chapel measures only 26 feet (8 metres) by 14 feet (4 metres) and in the nineteenth century was converted into a two-storey dwelling house. It was only in the 1960s, when scheduled for demolition, that it was rediscovered. By the strenuous efforts of the parish priest it was saved and restored and in 1968 reconsecrated.

Dover is a pleasant enough modern town now but it seems a pity that, having held such an important place in British history, more of the history has not remained visible.

Index